DON'T LET YOUR CONSCIENCE BE YOUR GUIDE

Don't Let Your Conscience Be Your Guide

by
C. Ellis Nelson

PAULIST PRESS
New York/Ramsey/Toronto

Library of Congress
Catalog Card Number: 77-94430

ISBN: 0-8091-2099-2

Published by Paulist Press
Editorial Office: 1865 Broadway, New York, N.Y. 10023
Business Office: 545 Island Road, Ramsey, N.J. 07446

Printed and bound in the
United States of America

Contents

To the memory of
Robert Francis and Joyce Hudson
Gribble

Introduction

"Let your conscience be your guide" is probably the most widely used rule of behavior. But when we ask what conscience is and why it has this authority, we can easily become puzzled. Ponder the following paragraphs.

All people have moral standards, yet standards differ from group to group. In some societies a man may have four wives, but in America a man may not have more than one wife at a time. In some countries oil and gas belong to the state, regardless of who owns the land. In the United States oil and gas belong to the owner of the land, and these minerals can be bought and sold separately from the land. If something is "right" in one society, why is it not "right" in others?

The internal regulator of morals is conscience; yet conscience gives different guidance to different people about the same thing. Some people give unselfishly of their time and money to make abortion available to any woman on the grounds that a woman has a right to decide what to do with her own body. Other people—equally sincere—form political organizations to make abortion illegal because they feel that every fetus

1

has a right to life. Why doesn't conscience tell us exactly what rules we should all follow?

Our conscience will often indicate what we ought to do in a given situation; yet we will not do it. Even the Apostle Paul experienced this inner agony. He confessed, "I do not understand my own actions. For I do not do what I want, but I do the very thing I hate." (Romans 7:15) On the other hand, our conscience will warn us not to do something, but we go on and do it anyway. Why is it that knowing what is good does not always cause us to do good, and knowing what is bad does not always cause us to avoid it?

We may feel guilty when we go against our conscience, but other people will do the same thing and not feel any discomfort at all. Shakespeare says, "Guilt will out," and in many cases he is correct. Most people can't stand guilt and they will do something to assuage their conscience. But there are still many people who cheat every chance they get and seem to feel the need to boast about their cheating rather than to confess. Why does guilt cause some people to lead fearful lives but seems not to penetrate the hard hearts of others?

Religion is considered to be the basis of good morals; yet there is no proven relationship between high ethical living and church membership. Social scientists have studied the ethical attitudes of people who were church members and those who were not. These studies seldom show church members to be greatly different from other people. This, of course, is a debatable point because these studies—especially if done with written questionnaires—may not be able to detect the relationship between religion and morals or be able to judge what people will do in an actual life situation. But leaving such evidence aside, we know this is a puzzling matter. On the one hand churches seldom lead society to new and higher levels of ethical living. On the other hand church people—lay and clergy—are often our most sensitive ethical leaders, and they give credit for their insight and stamina to the God they worship. Why can we not depend on religion to produce high moral standards always?

Introducing religion to a discussion of conscience adds further complications to our problem. If this were only an intellectual puzzle, we could play with solutions and move on to other interests. But conscience is an everyday matter that penetrates all our decisions and ceaselessly monitors our thoughts and wishes. And we who claim the Christian religion must have some idea of how it relates to conscience, or our faith will not be connected to the practical issues of life. So this is not an elective topic. Every person of almost every age level deals with it in some form. The only issue is how well we think through our position and how adequately we are able to shape our lives by our beliefs.

Knowing how important conscience is in moral development, I began a seminar in this field soon after I became a professor at Union

Theological Seminary in New York City. I have continued to offer such a seminar at Louisville Presbyterian Theological Seminary. To help students taking this seminar I edited a book of essays entitled *Conscience: Theological and Psychological Perspectives* (Paulist Press, 1973). Through these years I have developed my own position, and someday (first project for retirement!) I plan to write a full treatment. In the meantime I must be content to state in broad general terms what I have come to believe in these matters.

My Position

Many theologians have written on conscience, and some excellent treatments are available. Why another one? In addition to saying things my own way, I have tried to give special attention to the social sciences, especially depth psychology, sociology, and anthropology. Writers in these fields are not often quoted on this topic, but their approach to human development and their findings have been constantly in my mind. I used the social scientists to describe the human condition and to define stages of human development, for they do so with remarkable precision, clarity, and honesty. But my position is not an accommodation to a particular point of view within the social sciences. Rather, I have come to believe that the power of culture to shape beliefs and dictate moral behavior is so strong that only a revelation from God is capable of breaking through to give individuals a new lease on life and a concern to change the society in which they live. I suggest that such an experience should be called an "inversion" rather than "conversion," for it turns conscience upside down. The moralistic part of conscience becomes less dictatorial and the idealistic part in union with Christ becomes more and more the desire of one's heart.

ATTENTION

These lectures were written for ministers and seminary students with a theological background and some knowledge of the social sciences. Generally, I have avoided technical words and interesting bypaths. My purpose in these lectures was to outline a position in general terms; hence, there is not much documentation or elaboration. This makes it possible for the reader to decide quickly the merits of the overall argument. On the other hand, some important matters which normally would be brought out in a fuller discussion lie hidden in the text. Let me call a few to your attention.

—Guilt and shame are discussed as if they were distinct and separate feelings within the self. The reason for this is explained, but it is probably the case that the two overlap and within a person cannot be easily separated.

—Human beings go through stages as they become more mature, but the stages overlap. Also, some parts of the self may remain immature while other parts develop more rapidly than is normal. Only by obtaining a history of how a life has unfolded could we obtain some idea of why a person holds to his or her moral standards. I do not assume a stage theory of moral development that outlines separate steps—each higher than the other—as measured by some abstract principles.

—The term "religion" is used in such a general way that the context will at times imply any religion. In such places I am usually talking about the self and any religion that is presented to it. However, in most places I mean the Christian religion because that is the religion with which I am acquainted, and from the standpoint of conscience Christianity is a religion unless a person has an "inversion" experience.

—Some readers will have difficulty with my use of the term "faith" because I do not attempt to give it a formal definition. If the reader will note the way the term is used, a definition will be accumulated. Faith in God or Christ is thought of as being a certain kind of religious experience. The important thing is a definition of God and of how faith functions in life, and both of these are described in the lectures.

ACKNOWLEDGMENT

I deeply appreciate the invitation of Dr. Jack Martin Maxwell, President of Austin Presbyterian Theological Seminary, to give the Robert F. Jones Lectures in Christian Education. I have had many fine associations with Austin Seminary. I received my B.D. degree from this seminary in 1940 and at the invitation of the faculty started teaching Christian education part-time the next year. From 1948 to 1957 I served as Professor of Christian Education, and from 1966 to 1974 I served as a member of the Board of Trustees. The Robert F. Jones Lectures were inaugurated in 1949 during my tenure as professor. Dr. Jones, then as now, personifies the finest characteristics of a Presbyterian minister. He is a preacher of such merit that his sermons have been published. He is a leader of such reputation that he has served on many important church committees and as Chairman of the General Assembly's Board of Christian Education. And he is a pastor of such enduring qualities that he has served as senior minister of the First Presbyterian Church, Fort Worth, Texas, for the past 33 years. The endowment of this lectureship in his honor by members of his church shows their respect for his life and work.

I feel honored to give these lectures in 1978 during the 75th anniversary of Austin Seminary.

My personal association with the school spans more than half its history and, through my in-laws, almost all of its existence. You will notice that the book is dedicated to Professor and Mrs. Gribble, who were on the faculty from 1923 to 1960. Nancy Joy, their first child and my wife, grew up in a faculty home located where the administration building now stands.

For the purposes of these lectures footnotes have been used only when ideas or quotations were used in a direct way. If at a later time I am able to write a fuller treatment, more extensive documentation will be provided. In order to avoid as many errors as possible, I asked the following people to read the manuscript.

Frank Egloff, psychiatrist, Woods Hole, Massachusetts, has a special interest in the role of a congregation in forming and reforming faith in God.

Glenn Dorris, senior minister, Second Presbyterian Church, Louisville, Kentucky, has made a systematic study of conscience from a theological standpoint.

Eric Mount, Jr., professor of religion at Centre College, Danville, Kentucky, has placed conscience in the context of Christian ethics in his book *Conscience and Responsibility*.

David Ng, professor of Christian education at Austin Presbyterian Theological Seminary, Austin, Texas, has an expert knowledge of possibilities of moral education at each stage of human development.

The help of these friends is cheerfully acknowledged, although their views about conscience may not be—and probably are not—the same as my own. But for the purpose of trying to clarify this important area of our life, they were willing to offer me their constructive criticism.

C. Ellis Nelson
August 1977

Lecture One

The Roots of Religion and Conscience

Conscience is a curious and complicated internal power. Everyone is painfully aware of its presence. Its demands cause us to do strange and wonderful things. Its origin within the self is vague; yet its prompting can sometimes become a commanding voice. It is frequently fused with religion or a moral code; yet conscience is a part of persons who claim no religious faith. The folk saying "There is honor among thieves" illustrates the perplexing and universal characteristics of conscience.

Religion is no less complex. Anthropologists have never found a people without religion; but the forms of religion and their belief systems vary so widely that it is difficult to find many things on which they agree. Moreover, religion has many functions in human life. It can be a set of beliefs, a way of life, or a form of worship. In many cases religion is a person's allegiance to a particular church.

But in every case religion is intertwined with morality because religion always indicates what human relations ought to be and conscience is trained to enforce moral standards. Let us, then, analyze our Christian faith in relation to conscience in order to see how each affects the other and how faith in Christ is necessary for transforming conscience from a negative "watch-dog" attitude to a positive appeal to seek and do God's will.

To do this we must first turn from Christianity and conscience as social phenomena and look to the roots of our faith and morals. As long as we look at the visible manifestation of religion, we will see codes of conduct and creedal statements and lose sight of the motives for our behavior. We must answer the questions "Why are people religious and what conditions cause conscience to develop?" When we answer those questions, we will understand why some forms of Christianity are not sensitive to moral issues and why some forms of morality are more concerned to fill an individual's psychological needs than to seek ethical principles.

SELF-CONSCIOUSNESS

The human condition which produces religious faith and our inner governor of behavior is self-consciousness. Animals have some ability to reason and communicate; and some living beings, such as insects, have developed complex social organizations. But the animals and insects are not self-conscious. They do not have a means of recording or conserving their memories so that succeeding generations can develop a set of meanings from their experiences. Thus, animals exist in a form of life that is repeated by instinct generation after generation.

Self-consciousness and language are close together if, indeed, they are not two parts of the same process. We do not know much about the way these two things emerged in the history of humanity; but in the psychological development of the child, self-consciousness and language develop simultaneously. Self-consciousness in this sense is not exactly the same as ego formation. Psychologists studying child development have been able to detect signs of ego (a sense of self-hood) emerging a few months after birth. Self-consciousness develops later when the child is conscious of itself as a being separate from parents, when it is aware that its actions cause things to happen, and when it is able to comprehend the fact that living things cease to be. It is not possible to state exactly when this stage of development occurs, but a guess would be from the beginning of a child's use of words (about 18 to 24 months old) to the beginning of its interest in playing for extended periods of time with groups of children (to about four or five years of age). During this period the child achieves a sense of self as a separate person and—through the use of language—learns the lore of the people who nurture him or her.

The child is not completely self-conscious in this early stage, for there will be another intense period of introspection at the beginning of puberty when the self becomes aware that it is developing powers of reproduction. Moreover, the self must struggle internally for clearer identity throughout young adulthood and—in perhaps somewhat less intense form—until death. These latter phases of self-development, although important for the person, are a "finishing school" of life in comparison to the early stage of self-consciousness when the crucial issue of self-significance is set.

THE STORY OF EVERYONE

Let's run the risk of oversimplifying the human condition by describing it as the story of everyone. We can insert details and complications later. A child comes into self-consciousness slowly. He or she grows cautiously into a realization that there is death. How this happens we do not know. It must be related to the child's seeing people, animals, and plants die and a slow realization that all living things at some point stop being alive. An identification is made of the self as a living being, and somewhere in the young mind the hard fact asserts itself—he or she, too, will die.

Personal Source of Anxiety

Paul Tillich used to tell his classes, when they seemed perplexed by his insistence that knowledge of death was the beginning of self-consciousness, "Why, every child has faced the ontological question!" That comment brought laughter at the idea of a small child having an experience which a seminary student had difficulty understanding. However, I believe Tillich was correct. The best place to see and study this phenomenon is in a public park where mothers bring their two and three year old children to play. Sit quietly on a bench and observe the children. At some point a child will see an ant or a bug crawling. The child will look at it and then crush it with a finger or foot. When you see a child doing this for the first few times, he or she will most often stare at the dead bug. The child is learning the ontological lesson—what had life and movement now is lifeless and inert, and the action, which he or she controlled, made the difference. So the child learns two things: life can become lifelessness, and he or she is an agent with freedom to choose and power to carry out that choice.

These learnings are very deep in the mind and are mostly unconscious. That is why seminary students cannot readily remember that they have had these experiences. That is also the reason they laughed—to force adults to remember buried memories of their discovery of death is to awaken fears which the quick laugh is an automatic effort to placate.

These two learnings produce anxiety. To learn that one day we will no longer exist makes us restless and ill-at-ease. What happens when we die? Do we continue in some other form? The doctrine of immortality is a theological affirmation to heal the hurt which the self experiences when it learns about death. But even with the theological affirmation of immortality, the self is still anxious. General anxiety, that nervous apprehension that colors our whole life, is a heavy feeling of helplessness caused by our knowledge that life is slowly but steadily moving to an end.

To learn that we have freedom to cause death is but part of a wider freedom that we learn as we develop fuller self-consciousness. The child learns that it can choose one action or another. There is uncertainty as to which action is the one that is desired. Moreover, as the child grows, his or her mind grasps newer and ever-larger ideas of what can be done as the body comes more directly under the control of the conscious self. The tremendous mental and physical growth during the development of self-consciousness makes for more basic anxiety, for each additional bit of freedom brings with it the threat of failure. So the growing child is faced with a bitter dilemma that will continue throughout life. He or she is free to choose and act; but to choose and act may result in failure. However, *not* to choose and act would stifle the spirit and damage the self-esteem.

Thus, anxiety rides with every decision we make throughout life. For example, in choosing a marriage partner, the anxiety level may be so high it overwhelms a person. Another illustration is the politician who puts off crucial decisions as long as possible in order not to risk the wrong decision and makes excuses by pretending to "keep the options open." This means, of course, that the person doesn't know what to do; and the general anxiety about making a bad decision which may cause him or her to lose the next election is so great that a few tentative steps in several directions are made until a plan emerges as to how to move more decisively without too much fear of failure.

Anxiety, therefore, is the generalized feeling we have about our death and our freedom. As such, anxiety is to be seen as a condition of life. It is a condition of our humanity; and it is the basis of our psychic energy and creativity. Anxiety alerts us to new possibilities and challenges us to explore new ideas and to try different ways of living.

It is in this sense that we can say that anxiety is the normal companion of learning. Learning is the interweaving of knowledge and experience, and the learner has to be the weaver. The learner controls his experiences—or at least the reactions to the experiences—and every time of venturing forth to test what has been heard or to examine what is surmised to be true brings anxiety. The folk saying "Nothing ventured, nothing gained" is the equation for learning or for any other creative effort. And anxiety surrounds the whole enterprise. I have been using learning in the broad sense as anything that a person comes to accept as true. But the basic idea applies also to learning in the restricted sense of classroom instruction. New information, ideas, and facts are a threat to a pupil both in terms of what they are and in terms of the pupil's ability to understand them. That is why a classroom teacher must be careful not to make the threat of an examination or a performance too great, or the students may give up or may in some other way reject the challenge.

Anxiety as the Pre-Condition of Sin

As the growing child experiences the threat of death and the fear of misusing freedom, he or she reacts by doing things which will enhance the self or bolster the self-esteem. The child grasps for anything that will strengthen its ego. The struggle to affirm one's self, to prove one's own existence, is in direct ratio to the comprehension that one is a finite creature. Most of this takes place at an unconscious level of the child's mind. It is a primitive form of learning and reacting that fuses the emotions and the mental functions. Although the child will increasingly be able to think abstractly about religion, this will not begin to occur until about the age of eight or nine at the earliest; and the child's ability to think about religion in a reasoned way and have some understanding of the literary form in which the Bible is written will not occur until he or she is about twelve years of age. Thus, the earliest experiences of self-consciousness have to do with our total being. Only later are we able to get back to it with our reason and even then only with the greatest difficulty.

Why is this so? Because in this intense struggle, the self solves the problem of anxiety by actions we call sin. To enhance the self we depreciate others; to mask the temporary nature of our life we start to acquire things, taking them without regard to ownership; to escape detection we lie or blame others; to disguise our weakness we brag about our strength and skill. Anxiety, as Reinhold Niebuhr pointed out, is not sin, but it is "the internal pre-condition of sin."[1] The experience of sin is painful, and we seldom want to bring it out in the open. Rather, we try to handle it in some other way, as we shall discuss in the next lecture.

I am using the theological word "sin" because

it is the correct term; but if one insisted on secular language at this point, one could say the small child engaged in antisocial behavior. However, sin is the better word. It is the Biblical word; and sin describes disobedience to God, with whom we have to be justified, whereas antisocial behavior only implies that the child is not properly adjusted to society. Sin is different from antisocial behavior in that even God sometimes seems antisocial! God, according to our earliest Biblical stories, is in violent opposition to many social practices. Amos, Isaiah, and other prophets depicted God as being in a rage against liars, dishonest merchants, rich landlords, and politicians who were more concerned with power than with justice. Biblically speaking, sin is the most serious human deviation; it is far more than merely antisocial behavior.

The Biblical story of the Fall is profoundly true to our modern knowledge of selfhood. Our earliest dim memories are of our state of innocence, in a Garden of Eden. And when we came into selfhood, we "fell" into our present state of sin. As Kierkegaard put it, "Everyone is his own Adam." We all, like Adam and Eve, become aware of our end; and then we grasp the tree of knowledge which will make us like God, a being who does not die. The basis of human sin is pride, that is, determination to out-smart God. Sin is aimed toward or against God, and the solution of sin in the Biblical idiom must come from God. Human beings might cure antisocial behavior, but they cannot absolve sin.

Social Sources of Anxiety

The story of *the* Fall and *our* fall is so vivid in the fused depths of mind and emotion of everyone, and the resulting anxiety is so powerful and persuasive, that we seldom explore the social sources of anxiety. The anxiety which originally was formed in our innermost being by self-consciousness is reinforced and enhanced by our experiences as we grow older and have to take on broader responsibilities. We have only to list experiences that are common in our industrial, technical society to feel the force of externally generated anxiety. Unemployment is perhaps the greatest threat in our work-oriented culture. The Great Depression of the early 1930s seared the emotions of a whole generation, causing them to be unusually anxious about maintaining their jobs. Today, fear of unemployment is rooted in technological development which may make thousands of workers unnecessary. War and the threat of war revive our fear of death and disrupt our normal habits of life. Today the danger of nuclear explosion, set off by rockets from some mentally deranged ruler of a small country or by design from a large nation determined to rule, gives us anxious moments. Poisonous gas, which is stored all over the world by many nations, could escape by accident or irresponsible action and kill thousands of people—just as 6,000 sheep were killed in Nevada a few years ago when a shift in the wind carried the gas being tested in an unexpected direction. When one adds to this list of social conditions the normal problems of accident, disease, and assorted other ills that hit like lightning in a storm, one has a formidable array of external sources of anxiety.

The social and external sources of anxiety produce just as much sinful behavior as the personal sources. Threat of unemployment causes us to struggle to hold onto our jobs by aggression and often by deceitful moves against others. Some of the threat of unemployment and retirement is placated by Social Security and pensions, but even so only the physical needs are cared for. A person's sense of worth is not ministered to by pension plans.

The nasty side of humans was much in evidence a few years ago when the threat of nuclear attack caused states on our northeastern coast to urge citizens to build underground survival shelters. People who built the shelters had to decide whether they would stock their shelters with a shotgun in order to drive their neighbors away from the shelter in the event of a bombing attack! We need not continue this line of discussion; it should be clear that there are many threats to our existence from without which aggravate or increase the anxiety that is already within the self.

Hostility

Perhaps enough has been said about human beings to show that our anxiety creates a sinful condition. We should not stop our analysis too quickly, however. Just after the Fall, God announced that Adam, because he tried to become like God, was to be sent forth from the Garden of Eden "to till the ground from which he was taken." (Genesis 3:23)

Conscious of death and aware of freedom, every person will struggle all through life to hold on to what that person *knows* will finally be lost. Moreover, the symbol of an angel holding a flaming sword at the gate of the Garden of Eden to prevent Adam from coming back shows how radically each of us knows there is no going back to innocence.

The second Biblical story about humanity is as profound for our purpose as the first; for the story of Cain and Abel (Genesis 4:1-16) is the account of every person in society. When people live together, hostility is the generalized condition. Why? The answer seems to be that there is no way to raise a child except by some form of restraint. That is, a child has to be "socialized"; he or she can't have everything when it is wanted. Whatever the method of training—whether by spanking, confinement to a playpen, or verbal threats—it is a restraint. Moreover, in our modern world there are many dangers—electricity, machines, cars, medicines—which a small child can't understand; so the adults have to force patterns of behavior on the child just to keep the child out of physical harm. The child reacts to these restraints and frustrations with hostility.

When children are raised with other children, jealousy is the common experience. Each child wants the love of the parents to help overcome the growing self-consciousness; when this love has to be shared, there is often the feeling on the part of one child that it is not as acceptable—as loved—as the other. Acute hostility may, as in the case of Cain, lead to murder. Less acute cases lead to fights and other acts expressive of the dynamic tension which separates the siblings. The Biblical way of describing this tendency is that "sin is couching at the door," and the admonition "Its desire is for you" is a graphic way of recording the basic human condition of hostility. Although we may not like the stark simplicity of this story, who can show that the history of society is anything but a documentation of this basic trait? In certain small groups (such as the family, clan, or religious community) there are ways of building deep feelings of love and mutual concern that will, to some extent, bridge this gulf of natural hostility or that will mediate effectively between feuding persons. But in society at large we have only law, which is based on force of arms. Society can no more be our true home than can the Garden of Eden with its lost state of innocence.

CONSCIENCE

The story of humanity, told in these broad sweeping statements, leaves us with an understanding of human beings as creatures with deep feelings of guilt and shame because of having acted aggressively or vindictively against others. Like Cain, we feel that "my punishment is greater than I can bear," that we so deserve punishment for our sins as to need a special mark from God to protect us from those whom we have wronged. We must now explore more precisely the way the moral life is experienced and how Protestants interpret this experience religiously.

Carl Heim has said that Protestantism is a "religion of conscience." By this he must mean that Protestantism, after its historic break with the Roman Catholic Church in the early 16th century, turned most of the responsibility for the Christian life back to the individual. Thus, the inner court of moral authority, the conscience, becomes the central concern of Protestants. It is certainly true that some Protestant theologians take the position that conscience is

. . . the ineradicable witness to God in the heart of man: it is an independent inner condition of man's responsibility to God for his conduct; and it is planted in his very being by the Creator himself. . . . God has not permitted man to separate himself completely and absolutely from his Creator. . . . Conscience is the bond which preserves a connection between God and man.[2]

Many other writers use less precise language; yet when their backs are to the wall and the fighting becomes serious, they use the ultimate weapon—the Kantian dictum that the starry heavens above and the moral law within witness to the existence of God.

For others, conscience is the voice of God as described in these words:

We can, therefore, define conscience as that knowledge or consciousness by which man knows that he is conforming to moral law or the will of God. Our conscience tells, therefore, not only what we are but also what we ought to be.[3]

The affirmation that conscience is the basis of a practical ethic, a built-in regulatory device which, properly understood, will guide us safely through the stormy waters of decision, is widely held in Protestantism. Maurice is sure that conscience is simply "that in me which says, I ought or I ought not."[4]

Indeed the folk saying "Let your conscience be your guide" is probably the most widely believed and most deeply held ethical guideline among Protestants. But how valid or valuable is conscience as a guide? Should we Protestants allow our religious faith to rest on conscience as the basic moral reality? An examination of how conscience is formed will show why we must be wary of conscience as the voice of God, the proof of God, or the basis of a practical ethic.

The Formation of Conscience

Adolph Portmann has a striking statement about why so much comes to the baby from society. A person's birth is physiologically a premature birth, Portmann says. By this he means that not until the end of one full year of life is a baby as mature as most mammals when they are born. More than any other living thing, a human being is shaped by the environment. Society, or the "given" in life, is represented to the baby by its parents, especially the mother. The baby soon learns that there is an order of things that must be followed in order to get love and approval; there are other things that must not be done in order to avoid disapproval and punishment. The baby's morality is based on authority—an external "given"; yet the relationship is also one of love, for the baby is loved and fondled. As the little one grows, the regulatory authority is internalized and conscience is formed. In Freudian terms, this is the superego. As a child grows, much of its conscience becomes unconscious and restrictive. Perhaps we should, for purposes of this paper, call this the negative conscience. In this sense, conscience is extremely moral; for, when that internalized code is violated, guilt is precipitated and this happens even when the process is going on in our unconscious mind. The capacity to develop a conscience is innate, but the content of conscience will come from society.

Later, the child accepts the more positive principles by which the parents live; and these are internalized in an area of personality which is referred to as the ego-ideal, or, for purposes of this lecture, the positive conscience. These positive principles are more accessible to the ego than the negative conscience. Why? Perhaps it is because the negative conscience is formed first and therefore lies deeper in the personality. Perhaps the baby, when spanked, corrected, or restrained, thought that there was something wrong with it as a self rather than with its actions; perhaps the baby did not realize that the parents could *love*, even if they had to *correct*. All of these explanations have been offered to help us understand why the negative conscience is much more powerful than the positive and why it was driven underground, into our unconscious mind.

The negative conscience is restricted because it is trying to avoid guilt, and guilt is a reaction we cannot stand because our negative conscience expects punishment or disapproval. The positive conscience is expansive and is more open to education because it partakes of the conscious goals with which we associate our well-being. Not to live up to our goals creates shame, but shame does not have to be expurgated as guilt does. Shame causes us to want to do better, to rethink our situation, or to regroup our efforts to try again.

Conscience is, therefore, the word we use to describe a profound human experience. Without this experience we are subhuman or dimly aware of our situation. With this experience we are anxious and are permeated with feelings of guilt and shame for acts for which we know ourselves to be responsible. We must now turn to a more detailed examination of how conscience works in order to gain a clearer idea of how the Christian faith is, and is not, related to this basic human phenomenon.

Lecture Two

The Unreliability and Inadequacy of Conscience

The experience of becoming self-conscious, as we described it in the last lecture, creates a general state of anxiety and hostility which results in acts of sin. These sinful acts produce feelings of guilt and shame so powerful that a person is restless until these gnawing feelings are handled in some way satisfactory to the particular formulation of his or her inner life. For many Protestants—both trained theologians and the laity—the whole matter is seen in terms of conscience as a divinely installed regulatory device which reminds us of our duties and "hurts" when we do wrong.

Until fairly recently in the history of Christian theology, there has been little evidence that this conception of conscience was deficient. But our modern knowledge of the development of conscience will not allow us to make an easy identification between Christian faith and conscience.

THE UNRELIABILITY OF CONSCIENCE

It Develops as a Result of Training

The first reason why conscience is an unreliable basis for Christian faith is that it is a natural phenomenon, present in all normal people as a part of the process of becoming self-conscious. Conscience is neutral; it is not an agency for or against any religious faith. Conscience is the internal judge that makes us feel guilty when we break the rules and produces a sense of shame when we do not live up to our expectations. Conscience can exist independently of any religion. In fact, a simple negative conscience can be developed in animals.

Our family dog, Rags, for example, had a workable negative conscience. Rags lived in the house with us most of the year and his assigned area was the entry hall, the kitchen, and a back porch. Mrs. Nelson would not allow him to come in the living room because his long hair would be shed onto the rug. To enforce her decree, she would spank him when she found him in the living room, pull him out, and place him in the hall, telling him in a firm voice not to go in the living room. Our children, on the other hand, had no such rule for Rags; they would call him into the living room to play. Rags soon solved the problem. He would come in the living room if called or if he wanted to rest in front of the fireplace. However, before he would go in the living room under any condition, he would pause at the door to see if Mrs. Nelson were there. If not, he went in. If Mrs. Nelson was in the bedroom above the living room and started to come down the stairs, Rags got up and went out in the hall. Rags became so adept at this procedure that he could wake up out of a snooze while in the living room and trot out to the hall before he was caught.

Or, if we turn to the positive conscience—that part which develops later out of what the child more consciously accepts from the parents as what he or she really likes—we do not necessarily find this to support belief in God. Atheists and non-Christians have often developed a sensitive conscience and have demonstrated saintly lives by their high moral commitments. Mahatma Ghandi is but one of scores of people who have elevated the ethical level of life yet who did not adopt the Christian religion.

Its Moral Content Comes from Society

The second reason why we must not too quickly embrace conscience as an ally of faith is its social origin. Durkheim has said that the content of conscience is social. By this he means there is no other source, given the way conscience is formed, for the code of conscience to be formulated except that it comes from the culture in which the person lives. This is such an obvious affirmation today it is strange that we have to make it, but we must. Until sociologists and psychologists in our modern period began to investigate human behavior in a systematic way in various parts of the world, we seldom — if ever — faced the question of how human beings incorporated within themselves the behavior of their culture. Rather, we just observed that the style of life of other people was different; and, compared to our own, we usually found the behavior of other people to be deficient. Cannibalism and polygamy, for example, were labeled "wrong" without asking how persons born into a cannibalistic culture turned out to be cannibals.

The content of conscience — that which is considered to be right or wrong — is socially inherited. The family, small primary group, clan, or other communal society works out norms for human behavior, and these are absorbed by the small child long before the child can critically evaluate them or modify them to any extent. Thus, we can see that the formation of rules of conduct is one of the major things the church does for and with its members. The church, both locally and in its denominational program (especially in the formal curriculum materials of the church school) is a beehive of verbal activity, most of which is about situations considered to be right or wrong. This incessant norming of conduct is then transmitted to children through family and friends to give content and direction to conscience.

This description of the process of norming conscience should be accepted as one of the first duties of the church. We must not flinch from the responsibility. Our problem is that we have been unable effectively to separate ourselves from the culture enough to be critical of our culture. We have not only our own culture to transcend, but also we have to see through the culture of the Biblical writer to get the meaning of a passage for our own day. Of the two cultures that have to be interpreted, and to some extent transcended, the contemporary culture is the overpowering one. It is relatively easy to read the book of Philemon and see through the cultural form of slavery, because slavery was common throughout the Mediterranean world. It is extremely difficult for us to look at our own life and see that through our economic policies we are still maintaining a form of slavery in our own industrial society.

The long history of racial prejudice carried along in the church and by the church need not be repeated. The church's record in general is no better or worse than that of any other organization, such as a labor union. And that is my point. General cultural values generated by response to particular social and political problems form a frame of thought and attitude through which life is seen. Retailed in homes and small groups, the cultural values—when used to view the past or the Bible—normally interpret ideas or events from the Bible to fit the present. Thus, present day thought-forms are so pervasive and so deeply embedded in our minds that it is not unfair to say that much of our Biblical interpretation is more of a commentary on the commentator than it is an honest effort to find out what the passage meant to the writer. Since the emotionally charged attitudes about what is right and wrong flow spontaneously from the culturally conditioned conscience, we must be skeptical about an uncritical use of the phrase "Let your conscience be your guide."

Its Dynamic Quality Comes from Parents

The third reason why conscience is unreliable for developing the Christian faith is due to the process by which it is formed. It is surprising that an element of personality as well known and active as conscience has remained unexamined so long. It was not until 1917, when Freud was trying to discover the reasons for melancholia, that he formulated the idea of "identification" as the mechanism by which a person appropriates internally the values of the people who raised him or her.[1] Freud continued to work on this concept and gradually came to the conclusion that the process of "identification" was the way the superego and the ego ideal were formed. This term "identification" was taken over by social scientists and clinicians to explain the origin of extremely complex human behavior, such as personality traits related to sex, self-control, self-criticism, aggression against others, and guilt feelings, and a wide variety of adult behavior patterns, such as conscious efforts to resist temptation, labeling actions "right or wrong," or quoting general rules to guide conduct. Most, if not all, of these behaviors learned through identification are related to conscience or are formed in the person about the same time. But this mechanism of identification, although widely used to explain the origin of conscience, was not systematically investigated until Robert Sears and his associates at Stanford University's Laboratory of Human Development began a study in 1958. The findings, published in 1965, support the general theory of identification. However, the study has just opened up the field for critical inquiry, and it will be decades before we can speak with confidence about the exact process by which conscience is formed in an individual.[2]

In the meantime, we shall have to depend on the general formulation of the identification theory and the findings of Sears and his associates to describe how this structure of self-regulating behavior is developed. *Primary identification* is the process by which the child, up to the age of about four or five years, learns to behave like its parents. It is thought that the child is motivated to learn from the parents because of its dependent status.

This development assumes that the earliest relationship between infant and mother is a caretaking one. The mother provides constant biological support for the child's needs; i.e., she nurtures him, and he in turn becomes both physically and emotionally dependent on her.[3]

Sears' idea is that babies quickly learn that parents, especially mothers, do good things for them. When hungry, they are fed; when wet, they are dried; when sick, they are nursed; when comfortable, they are amused. Babies and small children like this relationship and imitate the general behavior of parents because the parents are the source of all good things. Also, babies have little, if any, experience with other adults; so they accept and absorb the behavior patterns and style of speech and thought of their parents long before they see or understand that other patterns are possible.

Sears also explores *secondary identification*, which was first proposed by Freud. This is a mechanism that develops later and—in Freud's work—is limited to boys. The theory is that the boy, because of his jealousy of the father who gets the attention of his mother, has strong ambivalent feelings toward the father. The boy likes his father, but he also wishes to be rid of the father's competition for his mother's affection. Not being strong enough to handle this problem, the boy gradually internalizes the nature of his father. In other words, he defends himself by becoming like his father. Sears' research data indicate that boys sometime about the age of four have begun to pattern their lives according to a masculine map; but whether it is caused by secondary identification will have to be determined by further research.

This brief description of research efforts to identify and describe the process of identification by which a child internalizes the parents' personality is enough for our purpose. It shows that conscience—broadly speaking—is intimately related to one's personality and that this process, in its beginning, is a spin-off from parents, especially mothers. These findings are not surprising, for all who have raised children or have observed children in their early years have seen this process at work.

This process of identification with parents as the normal and natural way for conscience to be formed makes for several problems in the development of Christian faith. One example is the church members who constantly refer back to the way things were done when they were children, indicating that their religious impulses are still fused with those of their parents.

A high percentage of teenagers who have been raised in the church drop out—or drop formal affiliations—when they go to college. The reasons for this common situation are varied. In some cases we might surmise that the teenager, going through puberty and entering an apprenticeship into adulthood, is emotionally thrown back to infancy. Just as in infancy reality was tested and adapted to, so the teenager is now testing reality again; however, this time he or she struggles alone to find the self amid the welter of conflicting impulses that rise within the new experiences. The teenager brings to this new reality-testing the content of the conscience that was spun off the parents. Religion—to the extent that it is a practical matter relating to behavior—is usually equal to the content of the conscience; and as the teenager goes through a rebellion against the parents to discover the self, he or she often drops the code and the religious symbols of that code.

This teenage rebellion is desirable in order for the person to develop self-identity apart from the parents. It is cited here to show that the process of identification may start a child's religious life; but it is not a satisfactory basis for an adult's understanding of and faith in God.

THE INADEQUACY OF CONSCIENCE

Conscience is inadequate for a life of faith because of the way conscience defends itself. The negative conscience is concerned only to discharge its guilt. Guilt has only one goal: equilibrium of the self. The threshold of tolerance of guilt is different for different people. One person with a sensitive conscience will walk three blocks to return a dime received by mistake; another person will gleefully keep the dime. Whatever the level of the threshold of guilt, every person has a way of dissipating feelings of guilt and shame. The way these feelings are discharged or handled is a clear indication of the place and significance of religion in this individual's life, because guilt can be dissipated in secular as well as religious ways.

We start, then, with the proposition that guilt and shame (but particularly guilt) are impossible to contain or ignore. Guilt will come out in some form. Normally, it is in vague feelings that the self can regulate by one of several mechanisms we shall discuss in a moment. In extreme cases, guilt is observed as "conversion hysteria": when a person's defenses are very vigorous, the guilt is turned unconsciously into some physical disability that hurts or hinders life and thus satisfaction is achieved without the conscious mind being aware of the transaction.

A few years ago the *Texas Medical Journal* published several such cases. One gave the account of a teenager in Dallas who, on coming out of a movie theater on a Sunday afternoon, found her arm had become paralyzed. After days of examination in a hospital, no evidence of illness or disease appeared. Then a kindly physician talked with her and found that she belonged to a very strict religious sect in which there was an inexorable law against going to movies on Sunday. The teenage girl, caught between her need for peer group approval and her religious prohibitions, had a conflict of conscience which was solved by the guilt's conversion into physical paralysis. The negative conscience was thus satisfied and equilibrium was restored within the girl's self; for it took that much punishment to fit that much disobedience according to the algebra of her own personality.

Many cases of this nature could be cited, but I shall not give more because they move our discussion into the abnormal. This one case is reviewed only to illustrate the power of conscience and to show that guilt demands and receives pay for exactly what it considers to be owed. The amount that is owed varies with the threshold of tolerance which has been established in the life history of each person. The manner of payment is normally through one or more mechanisms or strategies which discharge the obligation. These strategies are psychological; that is, they operate because that is the human way to handle guilt. But they are also deeply intertwined with our Judeo-Christian tradition.

Psychological Mechanisms

Let us examine some of the major mechanisms the self has devised to handle guilt.

Self-Punishment. Self-punishment is the classic way to discharge guilt, as the case of the teenager with the paralyzed arm shows. Psychologists commonly believe that some accidents occur and some unfortunate events happen because we unconsciously want them to happen. Beneath the level of consciousness, our guilt is causing just the right amount of inconvenience and pain to balance the account within our inner self. "Accident-prone" people are thought to be people who have an uncanny ability to work out their guilt problems in suffering caused by tragedies that might have been avoided.

In our Christian era, self-punishment was soon incorporated as a way of handling guilt. Simeon Stylites climbed a tower and sat there for years dispensing spiritual advice. People came to hear him speak, thinking he was unusually holy because he had taken on such an austere style of life. We have a long history of people who have beaten themselves, put on hairshirts, deformed their bodies, or in other ways punished themselves for their guilt.

In our church life there is probably more work and activity motivated by a desire for punishment than we care to admit. Serving on committees, washing dishes, even listening to sermons can be psychologically a punishment we want or need to keep our life on an even keel!

Also, those of us who help with the educational work of the church know that when the time comes to recruit teachers for the church school, we find ourselves using subtle ways of making prospects feel guilty if they don't accept.

Although we don't do this as a conscious tactic, we naturally develop this approach because we have learned how quickly the fear of guilt will motivate a person to accept a teaching assignment.

Partial Restitution. Partial restitution is a method of handling guilt by doing things that have a high valence of goodness attached to them, thus allowing us to continue to do things in other areas that produce guilt feelings. Once on a citrus fruit plantation in the Rio Grande Valley, I saw among the beautiful orange trees a series of hovels made of used railroad ties. I asked the owner what they were for. He replied that they were houses for the Mexicans who tended the trees. When I commented that the houses did not look adequate for that purpose, he replied that they were sturdy houses—much better than they had in town or in Mexico—and that, furthermore, living in the country among the trees was healthy. Moreover, he continued, he had a lot of interest in their spiritual well-being and had contributed to the building of a new church for the Mexicans so they could feel "at home" when they worshipped!

Denial of Guilt. Denial of guilt is one of the most subtle and primitive forms of discharging guilt feelings. When we do something that causes guilt, we almost automatically deny that we are doing it, or we justify our action by saying that we are doing it for the good of the person or the groups we are exploiting. When Nazi Germany started its expansion in 1938 by occupying Austria, the German nation was told it was being done for the good of Austria, since Austrians could not govern themselves properly. When we took over special rights for the Isthmus of Panama in the early 1900's prior to the construction of the canal, we said we were doing it to stabilize their government.

Ritual. Psychologically, ritual reduces guilt feelings. Exactly how this works is far from clear, but apparently any act or series of acts can become ritualized and in the process may placate anxiety. Almost any textbook in psychology will give illustrations of homemade rituals that persons suffering from compulsive neuroses act out to help maintain their emotional balance. Taking off one's clothes in a certain order, touching objects in order at certain times, following regular paths to shops or work, or other stylized forms of habitual activity will for many people be effective in holding down guilt.

When this basic activity of ritual is fused with a certain form of worship in which forgiveness of sins is an important part, then we have a significant device for handling guilt in the church. Let us leave aside for the moment the truth of forgiveness as a part of Christian worship and just reflect on the psychological fact. Consider, for example, the following situation. It is fairly common for a young minister after finishing seminary to arrive at a first parish and observe that the order of worship is not according to the best forms of worship learned in the seminary. Since this is a matter on which the new minister is informed and since he or she is the leader of worship, the order of worship is changed without further ado. The prompt negative reactions far exceed the importance of the move, and the young minister is baffled at the hornet's nest which has been disturbed. It makes no difference what the accustomed order of worship has been: if it is abruptly changed, you will know that you have hit some dynamic element in the people's lives. That dynamic element is the natural power of a set, ritualistic pattern to hold down anxiety. The people's reaction is not occasioned because they are old or Presbyterian or stubborn but because the accustomed ritual was a part of their overall efforts to control their guilt.

"Scapegoating." Scapegoating should probably have been listed first, since it has such a long history of usefulness in managing guilt. The term itself comes from the Old Testament. Leviticus 16 is but one of many passages in the Old Testament devoted to ways of removing guilt. In this chapter, the Lord tells Moses exactly how Aaron is to come into the holy place and precisely how he is to dress and handle himself as he selects, kills, and uses animals for the sin offering. The blood is sprinkled in important places to symbolize the cleansing of all of Israel; and at the climax of the ceremony, Aaron is told to "lay both his hands upon the head of the live goat and confess over him all the iniquities of the people of Israel, and all their trans-

gressions, all their sins; and he shall put them on the head of the goat, and send him away into the wilderness . . ." (v. 2). This ceremony must have been enormously effective. It combines a highly stylized ritual, including the killing of animals as a symbolic substitute—death for those persons who deserve death, the strategy of projecting the sin onto something outside themselves and then sending it away, out of their lives forever.

Thus, scapegoating has entered our vocabulary as a method of avoiding guilt by projecting guilt onto someone or something else. Psychologically, putting the guilt on someone else allows us the opportunity to hate or blame that individual, thus discharging our emotions while our rational faculties justify it. It is a strange procedure, but one of our oldest strategies for dealing with guilt.

Racial, ethnic, or religious prejudices often provide examples of scapegoating. Christians, for example, have a long history of anti-Jewish prejudice. One has only to sample the literature from the Medieval period to find illustrations of the way Christians prohibited Jews from practicing many vocations and professions but allowed them to be moneylenders. Christians prior to the Reformation believed it sinful to accept interest on money loans. This brought about a situation whereby the Christians in the Medieval period put the Jews into banking and then vented their hostility on the Jews because they were bankers!

The whites' treatment of the blacks is another vivid illustration of scapegoating. The exploitation of the blacks during slavery was so obviously inhuman and degrading that whites built up an elaborate defense against the guilt that was generated. Much of this guilt was discharged by projecting it onto the blacks themselves and then blaming them for their condition. For example, whites would say that Negroes who were brought over as slaves were not civilized or that they were not fully human. Perhaps the worst form of this type of scapegoating was to appeal to the Bible for God's confirmation of this viewpoint. Using the story of Noah's drunkenness, it was pointed out that the word Ham, the name of the youngest of Noah's three sons, is a word that also means black. Thus, when Ham, according to the story, alerted his brothers about the father's naked, drunken condition, the brothers discreetly covered Noah. When Noah had sobered up and learned what had happened, he cursed Ham and said, "A slave of slaves shall he be to his brothers." (Genesis 9:24) A literal interpretation of this story makes all black races ordained by God to be slaves to the white races. This literal interpretation was a perfect scapegoating strategy, for it discharged guilt right back to God himself.

In more recent times, racial scapegoating has taken a different turn. Now that the blacks are moving into the mainstream of American society, it is being said, without any research evidence at all, that blacks cannot learn readily, and this attitude is used to justify poor schools for blacks. As blacks began to run for important political offices or developed their own businesses, we often heard whites say that the blacks did not have the experience necessary for such responsibility. These people were trying to justify a psychological strategy for maintaining their prejudice against blacks.

Social Mechanisms

These personal strategies for handling guilt may be enough to illustrate the phenomenon, but there is one more strategy that should be mentioned. Lacking an approved technical name, I shall call it "social acquiescence." Although it has its origin in the individual psychological makeup, the manifestation of this strategy is so clearly social that it deserves a special classification.

Social acquiescence is the process whereby a person gives up responsibility for some of his or her actions by self-identification with a well-defined, socially approved norm of behavior. When this happens, the individual actually assigns a part of the conscience to the collective will and then feels little guilt when orders are executed from that collective will which, in fact, may go against his or her own personal norm of conduct.

This process of handling guilt by social acquiescence was shown in dramatic terms at the Nuremburg trial of Nazi war criminals. Dr. Lee

Alexander, a psychiatrist stationed at the trial to observe the procedure from a psychiatric point of view and also one who interviewed prisoners, stated that a number of the worst offenders against common decency were some Nazis who were charged with the most barbaric acts and who seemed to have no feeling of guilt about what they had done. It soon developed that these officers had so identified themselves with the Nazi party that they had abandoned their own wills to the will of the party and could execute party orders without a feeling of guilt over acts they knew to be wrong.

The same process was observed some years ago when the U.S. Justice Department sued General Electric and Westinghouse Corporations for price-fixing. The suit was against officials of those corporations for their actions in fixing the prices on bids and not allowing the free enterprise system of competing prices to operate. The lawyers for the corporation officials who were on trial argued—just as lawyers for the Nazi officials did—that their clients were part of a huge organization and that these men were only following orders. The corporation executives were simply doing what the system expected and were, in their private lives, men with high moral standards and, in many cases, active church workers.

We must not let the spectacular nature of those illustrations obscure the principle underneath, namely, that when a social group has clearly defined norms of conduct and purposes, members of the group have a tendency to subordinate their private judgment to the will of the group. This is the reason why a group can act more severely than a person, why a nation acts more cruelly than a local community. Perhaps the larger organization or the nation is engaged in activities that would normally make us feel guilty, but by the process of social acquiescence we handle our guilt and do not offer an effective protest. In a sense, social acquiescence is a form of projection. Society, the system, or the establishment becomes the scapegoat on which we project our guilt.

Looking at this array of ways the negative conscience handles its guilt feelings and at the intimate way these mechanisms may or may not be intertwined in religion reveals several problems. The fact that many people can handle their guilt without religious beliefs shows that conscience can be separated from faith. But more important for us is the way the Christian religion has become for many people simply a way of handling conscience, not a way to know or try to understand God. The negative conscience is only interested in saving the ego of the self—not in trying to enlighten the self. The self that handles guilt isn't getting anywhere; it is simply surviving and functioning. This is no small accomplishment, given the power of guilt to destroy the self; but it is not a big thing, either.

Perhaps our most serious problem of conscience at work is the easy way in which a church member can appropriate out of the theology of the

Christian faith just those articles of belief which provide medicine for a hurt conscience. This grabbing of a few beliefs such as "Christ died for our sins" will psychologically relieve the symptoms of the illness; but will they introduce the person to a life of faith in God? An answer to that question will form the substance of our next lecture.

Lecture Three

The Inversion of Conscience

We have, perhaps, done enough to show that conscience is an unreliable and inadequate basis for the Christian faith, though we must establish this point clearly or even exaggerate it before we can begin to see how radical the faith of a Christian is. The negative conscience is so powerful that it will work out guilt feelings in many kinds of human behavior, including religious behavior; so we must identify it clearly, or we will continue to confuse the negative conscience with the Christian faith. Let us now move away from the individual and look at four common patterns of religious behavior found among Christians who seem to be motivated by conscience rather than by faith in God.

Robert K. Merton introduced into the literature of sociology the terms "manifest functions" and "latent functions" of human behavior. He used these terms to clarify what keen observers of human behavior have been saying for a long time—namely, that there are discernible differences between the overt, conscious, describable patterns of human activity and the covert, perhaps unconscious, and rather indescribable motives for this activity. Moreover, there is no clear, positive correlation between motives and human activity. A group of people, for example, may all be engaged in the same activity, such as playing baseball, but there may be a dozen or more motives which energize the players.

This conception of manifest and latent functions helps us understand why some groups who manifestly appear to be doing one thing that doesn't seem to be significant are actually motivated in a latent manner by other needs and desires. Merton cites the Hopi Indian ceremonies designed to produce rain. To an outsider this is a superstition. One can't understand why the Indians continue the ceremony, since it seldom produces rain. But if one looked for latent functions, one could surmise that the Hopi Indians conducted the ceremonies because they met other needs: the rain dance provided an opportunity for the tribe to express its group identity and for individuals to find and refresh their selfhood in relation to their deep memories of what a Hopi Indian is.[1]

A common illustration is teenagers who have just received their driver's license. They find all kinds of manifest functions, such as going to the grocery store, mailing letters, or going to church—in the car, of course. We know also in this situation that in our culture there are powerful latent functions at work: the teenagers' desire for independence; their growing concern to achieve adulthood, of which driving a car is a major symbol; and a yearning to control and use machinery.

More than a hundred million Americans claim to be members of a Christian church. The manifest function of their activity could be described as worship of God, seeking to know the will of God for their lives, or engaging in ceremonies and celebrations relating to their beliefs.

Would we say that the latent functions (that is, the reasons individuals participate in church activities) were always for these overt purposes? Motives for any human activity are complicated and are poorly understood because they often spring from the unconscious mind.

Using Merton's notion of manifest and latent functions, we can identify four forms of the Christian religion which are more related to the latent function of handling the negative conscience than they are to the manifest function of worshipping and serving God.

First there is a form of religion that helps a person avoid any personal experience with God. Think about God for a moment as God is discussed from our pulpits, in our church school curricula, and in most sections of the Bible. God has the image of a demanding being—one who expects believers to change their lives or to suffer. The great heroes of Biblical faith were people who were uprooted and sent by God on dangerous and lonely journeys or who were charged with a mission that left them naked, poor or despised by their neighbors.

The universal symbol of Christianity is the cross. Believers are told in the words of Jesus, "If any man would come after me, let him deny himself and take up his cross and follow me." (Luke 9:23) Moreover, we are told that it will be difficult to get into the kingdom of God if we have wealth (Matthew 19:23). We could go on to enumerate the great leaders from the Apostle Paul through Martin Luther King, Jr., and we would have before our eyes a parade of people involved in problems, difficulties, and assassinations.

This stereotype of God is not so much inaccurate as it is incomplete. A more balanced reading of the Biblical accounts would show that men of faith were often happy in their vocation. Their conviction that they were being used by God for his purposes was all the reward they wanted or expected. But the image of God as a jealous God who will not allow substitutes and as one who is most often struggling with his people to bring about a more righteous communal life is true.

How many of our hundred million Christians in America want what the Bible and church history indicate are the possible and probable results of faith in God? Not many. The way to avoid the consequences of what the Bible seems to require for faith in God is to be religious about what the Bible says. We do this by worshipping not God but the story of what God has done in the past.

This is done in ritual, in stained glass, in ornate houses of worship, and so on.

The cross, which was a crude arrangement of rough wood, we now make out of gold, decorate with filigree work and encrust with jewels. By making the cross esthetically pleasing, we are able to worship it and leave it.

In short, we want to have our cake and eat it too. Our "cake" is our life and we don't want to change it very much. We do not want to cause ourselves pain or discomfort, and, above all, we do not want or perhaps cannot bear critical comments from our neighbors.

All the while, our conscience hurts us for sins we have committed, and we must do something to dissipate the guilt. The conflict in ourselves is solved by associating ourselves with the church, where we have a gathering of people who believe in God. Then through the normal psychological mechanisms of handling guilt mentioned in the last lecture, we are able to achieve psychological equilibrium.

Second, the other side of avoidance is reassurance. In this form of religion, the guilty conscience is still the dominant element in the personality structure and the individual uses religion to handle it. After all, one of the oldest creedal statements in the New Testament is that "Christ died for our sins in accordance with the scriptures." (I Cor. 15:3) This creedal assurance, plus its elaboration in church theology and its centrality in the rite of baptism and the confession of faith for church membership, makes it the Christian doctrine par excellence. At this point I do not want to discuss the truth of the doctrine of forgiveness, but I want to call attention to those who wallow in it.

Our hymns of assurance reflect the *subjective* side of this doctrine. Think of the hymn, "Blessed assurance, Jesus is mine! Oh, what a foretaste of glory divine!" There is nothing in that poem but a grasping after reassurances. Not any idea is offered about what a person would become if he or she did "take hold" of Jesus. There is not the slightest suggestion that a person who had assurance from Jesus would also be expected to help build the kingdom of God. Looking at the matter psychologically, people who have to be constantly reassured that their guilt is taken care of are those who are not thoroughly convinced that their sins are forgiven. Perhaps that is why such people are often strong believers in the penal substitutionary theory of atonement. Deep within their being, they feel that sin must be punished—just as they have been punished for wrongdoing; and their reassurance is strengthened by insisting that the Son of God had to suffer on the cross. The equation deep within their being is this: someone must pay when guilt is felt, and Jesus' suffering is necessary for the guilt they feel within. Needless to say, people using Christian theology this way are in no condition to hear Paul when he says, "Present your bodies as a living sacrifice, holy and acceptable to God." (Romans 12:1) Their interest in God is limited to what God has done to relieve their guilt.

A third and more complicated function of conscience latent in religious forms is fear masquerading as good behavior. A small boy is given a code of things he is expected to do—many of which he does only because he is afraid of the results of disobeying his parents. This code of goodness, however it is formulated, stands over him as an "ought." This part of our personality, if left in its natural state, will fester and break out in spasms of hatred about the code of "goodness" that we are forced to follow. Karin Horney labeled this condition "fierce goodness."

A Biblical illustration of fierce goodness is found in the parable of the two sons. Luke records Jesus as saying the youngest son collected his inheritance from his father and went into another country where he wasted his money in loose living. After difficult days, he "came to himself" and returned to his father and asked for forgiveness. After the prodigal son had come home and a joyful banquet in honor of his restoration into the family was in progress, the elder brother returned to the house and heard music and dancing. "And he called one of the servants and asked what this meant. And he said to him, 'your brother has come and your father has killed the fatted calf because he has received him safe and sound.' And he was angry and refused to go in. His father came out and entreated him, but he answered his father, 'Lo, these many years I have served you and never disobeyed your command, yet you never gave me a kid that I might make merry with my friends.' " (Luke 15:26-30) Note the basis of his goodness: "I never disobeyed your command."

The elder son felt that he *had* to be good. He was good because he had been told to be obedient as a child, and he had never worked through this relationship with his father. He would not go in to the banquet even though his father was outside begging him to join the celebration. The pattern of his whole life had been shattered. He had done what his father wanted and had therefore expected a reward. His brother violated the rules and still got his father's blessing. Therefore, he felt tricked, used. Goodness, he thought, doesn't pay. The struggle in the self of the older son was with a section of his childhood conscience that had never grown up, that had never adjusted to the authority of the father. So the older son reacted as he did when he was a small boy: his response to his father was defiance. We need not push this matter further. We have all seen the person who always wanted his good acts noticed and catalogued. We have seen and we have probably all participated in goodness that was joyless and calculating.

The fourth form of conscience working latently within religion is casuistry. When the conscience is formed, as we pointed out in the last lecture, it is always about a code of conduct. The small child learns that certain things are forbidden and these acts stand within his or her conscience as law.

We must not look on this process as demeaning or as having negative value. It is absolutely essential for society that children learn that there is an order which has to be maintained. Otherwise, social life would be impossible. People have individual rights, and a basic respect for these rights is essential for any organized human accomplishment. In order for us to have our rights, we have to see that others are given their rights. In this sense, the problem of society is justice, that is, the prevention of capricious or arbitrary acts against individuals. That is why law—or basic moral regulations—defines what one person cannot do to another. The first punishment a child receives is usually about what he may not do. This becomes a moral code to him. This early punishment is an effort to define his limits and to teach the child what is considered wrong or unjust. It is for this reason that the sense of injustice with its natural and unconscious fear of punishment is much clearer in our mind than is the sense of justice or what ought to be.

It is no surprise, therefore, that moral laws are normally stated in the negative. The Ten Commandments, insofar as they relate to human relations, are things we may not do. The context of the Ten Commandments in Exodus 20 shows that they were intended as the irreducible minimum of moral obligation on the individual for the welfare of the nation. (See also Deuteronomy 4:1-14.) The laws were taught to children at every opportunity — at play, in the house, or while walking on errands (Deuteronomy 11:1-25).

Law is a complex idea, and it is not made any easier by the variety of meanings attached to it. We Americans usually think of law as legislative or positive law — giving requirements or prohibitions, such as the traffic light on the corner. In the Bible, law can have that meaning, too. But most often the word "law" is the English translation of Torah, which means teaching, guidance, direction, judgment, or even, in some cases, revelation from God. Torah was the general term for the whole counsel of God to the covenant people. To keep Torah was to be God's people in obedience to divine guidance. Israel's vocation was to be a blessing to all of the people of the world. Israel, by keeping Torah, would be God's showcase to the other nations of how wonderful life could be (Exodus 19:1-6, Genesis 12:1-3). Thus, Torah was to be the heart of a person's desire (Psalm 1:2), the center of worship (Psalm 19), and the object of personal meditation and thought (Psalm 11:9).

In many individuals, and in certain historical periods, Torah was the source of a sensitive and creative religious life in Israel. But we must note that Torah also became lifeless and was interpreted legalistically. Just when this happened, historically, it would be difficult to determine. I would guess that for many Israelites Torah became obligation almost as soon as Torah was developed, just as worship of the golden calf took place almost immediately after the revelation of the commandment to Moses that Israel should have no idols (Exodus 32).

How could teachings, believed to come from God, be converted to pedestrian laws? There appear to be two factors. One is found in the nature of any general truth or moral obligation such as the Ten Commandments. Specific cases develop which do not exactly fit the law. An interpretation becomes necessary. Law always has to be interpreted to fit cases and unusual conditions, so there is always a series of courts or judges for this purpose. Israel had courts, rabbis, and informal conferences of elders "at the gate" of the villages, who hashed over unusual problems. Gradually, there grew up interpretation of the law which had the force of law. This is a normal and necessary development.

Another factor is more directly related to the way conscience is formed. The tremendous experience between God, Moses, and the other leaders of Israel, which was shared, perhaps, by a sizable number of the common people, made Torah a glorious possession. But that formative experience could not continue as a creative experience. It left a residue of rules to be followed in order for the people to please God. The residue of rules, when taught to the children, would stand in their mind only as rules; and the experience which motivated the rules would only be a story of how things were with people in the past. This is the natural history of social revolution and wars of liberation. In order for the social gains of a revolution to be held, the ideology has to be taught to the children; but by the third generation the sanctions for the ideology seem unreal and the ideology itself becomes a regularized way of living. The drift is always from ideology to law, because children grow up in a new situation. Ideology, in fact, becomes law whenever it is taught as an "ought."

The code of conscience, therefore, is always at first a given, a series of commands that are to be obeyed. The word "command" is not too strong to describe this situation, for the young child absorbs the regulations as commands. Although people may modify the commands when they become older and are able to reflect on their behavior, they are seldom free from a twinge of guilt when they violate a command learned as a child. It is the phenomenon of obeying a command which has been interpreted in conscience as a code or of having to handle the guilt which comes from disobedience that sets up the situation for casuistry.

The first dictionary definition of casuistry is a "science or doctrine of dealing with cases of conscience and of resolving questions of right and wrong in conduct." This role of the judge—working out a just way to bridge the gap between the abstractions and generalities of law and the specific facts of a particular case—is necessary.

Casuistry in this sense is the Supreme Court of the human mind, and it should be held in high regard. But the second definition of casuistry as "sophistical, equivocal, or specious reasoning, especially in regard to law and morals" is the one that comes to mind because it is also a process of trying to beat the game, so to speak. The game is how not to break a law that is preventing us from doing something we want to do. An everyday illustration of this situation is the traffic stop sign. About the only people who ever come to a dead stop are people who are just learning to drive or people who are test-driving to get a license. The ingenuity of the human mind is no better demonstrated than when it is trying to glide by disliked prohibitions in order to avoid guilt.

Historically, the use of casuistry shows how conscience, the most dynamic part of our mind, interacts incessantly with our reason to produce a rationale for our conduct. Rationalization is our way of trying to avoid guilt by working our way around a prohibition. Perhaps the rule about the Sabbath is a good illustration of how the process works.

Originally, the fourth commandment, "Remember the sabbath day to keep it holy ..." (Exodus 20:8), was intended to make the Sabbath a holy day. Incidentally, the idea of taking one day in seven for rest and communal worship was radical. There was nothing like this anywhere in the ancient Near East. The idea that a servant or a slave would have one day off was considered ludicrous. Sabbath, for the Hebrew, was a practical way of saying that life was holy; it was a constant reminder of one's moral and spiritual obligations to God. Theologically, the idea of Sabbath is a beautiful and winsome statement of God's concern that each person's life be more than work, although work itself might be creative. However, the Hebrews by the process of casuistry began to domesticate the Sabbath, so that it would be manageable for their purposes.

You can see how this happened. What is work in relation to Sabbath? Would it be work to build a fire if the purpose was cooking on the Sabbath? What is travel in relation to Sabbath? Would it be work to visit a sick relative? A sick friend? How close would the relative have to be to qualify for an exemption? In the course of time the rabbis dealing with these questions developed an oral tradition consisting mostly of cases and judicial judgments about the Sabbath to guide the common man. The section on the Sabbath in the Talmud occupies two of the twelve volumes of that set of extended comments about the Ten Commandments. A reading of almost any part of the Talmud will show that the predominant problem of the rabbis was to make a judgment which would draw a line between acts that were satisfactory and those acts that were culpable—that is, deserving blame and guilt. One should read a part of the Talmud to get some conception of what the religious mentality of many Jews was in Jesus' day. We must be careful how we look back on this period and not label all Jews as legalists. After all, Jesus, Paul and almost all the disciples were Jews nurtured on the Torah. Yet, we must not disguise the fact that Jesus' greatest conflicts were with religious leaders and that the issue was the proper interpretation of the law. The Sermon on the Mount is a provocative challenge to the prevailing religious ideas. "For I tell you," Jesus is remembered to have said, "unless your righteousness exceeds that of the scribes and pharisees, you will never enter the kingdom of heaven." (Matthew 5:20)

When Jesus began to teach along those lines, the anger and anguish of the Pharisees quickened. Walking through a grainfield on the Sabbath with his disciples, Jesus picked some grain to eat. The Pharisees, who were apparently following him, criticized him for allowing his disciples to break the Sabbath law. Jesus reminded the Pharisees that King David and his hungry soldiers had, on one occasion, eaten the "holy bread"—indicating that in principle satisfying hunger was more important than the literal interpretation of the law. Then Jesus added the familiar words, "The Sabbath was made for man, not man for the Sabbath." (Mark 2:23-28) On a different occasion, while in the synagogue on the Sabbath, Jesus healed a man with a crippled hand. Again, the Pharisees announced that Jesus had broken the law, but Jesus' reply was almost irrefutable, "It is lawful to do good on the sabbath." (Matthew 12:9-14)

It is obvious from these few illustrations from the life of Jesus that he was defining what was good and ought to be done, while the dominant religious leaders were concerned about what was bad and how to avoid these actions. It is my contention that these two concerns spring from two different sources within the self. We shall explore them in more detail later. Here we are holding to the one major observation, that the code of behavior which is appropriated by the negative conscience is usually handled legalistically. We must not assume that Jesus' teachings put a stop to casuistry. The process went to work at once in the early church. For example, Paul began to preach the glories of the grace of God, who, through the sacrifice of Jesus, freed us from our sins. Some Christians in Rome were able to see that doctrine as a license to sin, in order that God could have the pleasure of forgiving them! (Romans 3:7-8; 6:1, 15)

This human proclivity to turn moral code into casuistry can be seen in many places in the history of the church. It is all around us today. When the penitential system grew up in the Roman Catholic church, handbooks of rules appeared so that priests could quickly assign obligations or duties in cases of infraction of moral laws. Calvinism, especially in Holland and New England, became legalistic. Today, those of us who preach and teach in the church know how often our people are curious about the meaning of faith *only* to the extent that it requires something of them; and then they just want to know how much they are expected to do or to contribute.

THE INVERSION OF CONSCIENCE

You have probably noticed that my method of analysis is descriptive. Starting with the experience of self-consciousness, we moved to the formation of conscience and have been examining the way the negative conscience (superego) produces and handles guilt, with or without religious orientation. We have examined the negative conscience in some detail because of its power and because it is the basis of so much of our religious life which is immature. I have stayed rather close to the psychological conditions which produce a pseudo-Christianity because that is where the trouble lies. Once we see that some forms of Christian religion are primarily ways individuals have devised for handling their negative conscience, then we know why these forms of Christian religion are so ineffective and irrelevant. The latent function overrides any manifest function of real service to—or concern about—society. That is one reason why so much of American Christianity is clannish, introspective, heaven-oriented, concerned about the past, or enamored of purely private virtues and stately buildings.

But that is not the whole story. At the end of

the first lecture, I mentioned that as the small child develops a conscience, he or she also internalizes attitudes and patterns of behavior which are seen as pleasing in parents or other nearby adults. The child voluntarily and gladly accepts certain beliefs about conduct that is really wanted and goals that are desired and pursues them with cheerfulness and rationality. This we have labeled the positive conscience or ego ideal. This portion of the personality is mainly conscious and accessible to the ego. Perhaps for this reason, or because it was formed later, it is weaker than the negative conscience. The content of the positive conscience is also social in that it is formed from whatever the parents had to offer. However, since the positive conscience is open to the conscious "I" of the self, it is open to growth, stimulation, new ideas, and new models of behavior.

When we violate our positive conscience, we experience shame. This is a different psychological reaction from the reaction to guilt.

Guilt, as we have indicated, is concerned with specific acts or thoughts that go against clearly understood regulations, and the feeling is handled by one or more mechanisms. The result of using these mechanisms is inner equilibrium, for that is all guilt wants or needs. But shame results from failure to live up to what one has voluntarily accepted and causes a person to be concerned with self. It causes one to think of why one did not do what should have been done and often leads to insight into one's own nature. The mind works through the quality of one's experience and moves voluntarily to change the self-image and the relations with others. In this sense, shame causes us to face our deepest self and—in a moment of self-revelation—it opens up our perception of our own possibilities. Real shame does not immediately prompt action so much as it makes for reflective thought which re-orients and re-educates the self. In short, shame brings about transformation.

The experience of shame is used throughout the Bible. The general idea in the Old Testament is that shame results when a person betrays God's trust. The worst shame, therefore, is idolatry (Jeremiah 2:26); for this is the ultimate betrayal of God. Contrariwise, the promise is made by the Psalmist that "none that wait for thee shall be put to shame" (Psalm 25:3).

The New Testament seems to carry this same general usage but probably goes further in relating shame more directly with glory. For example, in the fifth chapter of Acts, we find the Apostles in prison because of their vigorous preaching and healing. They are brought before the council and it appears that they will be killed, when Gamaliel intervenes with his wise and moderate words. The council, therefore, calls the Apostles in, has them beaten, and orders them not to speak in the name of Jesus. The account says, "They then left the presence of the council, rejoicing that they were counted worthy to have suffered dishonor (or shame) for the name" (Acts 5:41). The lack of a sense of shame is characteristic of the enemies of

Christ. Paul says of them, "Their end is destruction, their god is the belly, and they glory in their shame, with minds set on earthly things." (Philippians 3:19)

The phrase "Be not ashamed of Christ"—or its equivalent—is used by several New Testament writers (Mark 8:28, Luke 9:26, I John 2:28). In each case, the writer warns that we should not separate ourselves from Christ, which is a reverse way of saying that our glory is in our relationship to Christ.

Freedom from the Power of Sin

Paul's sudden and dramatic conversion is so well known we need not say very much about it. We do, however, often forget the element of time in Paul's experience; we fail to remember that, after his experience on the Damascus Road (Acts 9:1-19), Paul went to Arabia (Galatians 1:17) for reflection. This period of withdrawal is crucial for growth since re-orientation of the self is a slow process. Paul's conversion was used by the early church as a mark of God's guidance and an illustration of Christ's power to change lives (Acts 22:6-21; 26:12-18); yet Paul seldom refers to it in his letters (I Corinthians 15:3-8). Apparently, Paul did not care to absolutize the form of experience he had. Rather, Paul was concerned that the *theology* of his religious experience be preached and lived so that others could know the freedom he had obtained in Christ.

It is the freedom which Paul achieved and how he achieved it that we must note. We say Paul was converted, but that term no longer carries the proper connotation. Conversion has come to mean a change from one religion to another, or changing from one form of money to another. It is too restrictive a term for what happened to Paul and what needs to happen in our own lives. True, Paul was converted from Judaism to Christianity, but what went on in Paul's life was more than a switch in beliefs.

The word "conversion" has several liabilities; it is not descriptive of the psychological process through which one goes in order to have an authentic experience with God. Moreover, the word "conversion" is not often used in the Bible. The more frequent Biblical word is "repent," which in the gospels and Acts means literally that one must change one's mind around. Perhaps we should use the Greek word "metanoia" or an English equivalent term, "personality inversion."

Granted, the word "inversion" has liabilities; but its obvious meaning is "turning upside down" or "opposite in order"—and that is just what is important in this instance. A true religious experience, whether it is sudden or slow, reverses the order and power of the negative and positive consciences. The positive conscience, that which we consciously want to be and do, becomes dominant;

and the negative conscience, that which we feel guilty about, becomes recessive. This does not mean that sin is suddenly dismissed. Nobody in the history of Christian theology was more aware of the persistent activity of sin than Paul; but no one has been clearer than Paul in saying that sin is no longer able to control the life of a Christian. The Christian, according to Paul, is "no longer . . . enslaved in sin." (Romans 6:6) His sentence "So you also must consider yourselves dead to sin and alive to God in Christ Jesus" (Romans 6:11) is an exact description of the inversion that is necessary. For when that happens, then, ". . . You who were once slaves of sin have become obedient from the heart to a standard of teaching to which you were committed, and, having been set free from sin, have become slaves of righteousness." (Romans 6:17-18) Paul's phrase "once slaves of sin" is not too harsh; for the negative conscience has a slavish hold on our personality. What Christ offers is freedom from slavery to sin. (See Romans 2:12—3:31; Galatians 5:1; I Corinthians 8:12—9:2.)

Desire for Righteousness

Speaking in human terms as Paul does (Romans 6:19a), I would say that the inversion of the personality structure is not complete if it simply puts the positive conscience more in control. We must remember the positive conscience has a code, too. That code of conduct comes from the parents or other adults who nurture the small child. Moreover, the positive conscience is open to formation over a long period of time; and during early adolescence it becomes particularly susceptible to strong attraction to adults with whom the teenager has a satisfactory relationship. Such experiences are often creative and regenerative to the growing person, helping the younger one to define a mental image of the kind of person he or she wants to be. However, regardless of how psychologically healthy the process of self-definition may be, the content can be secular if the process does not move the person from attachment to parents to an emotional attachment to Christ.

Note that Paul's language says that the properly introverted person "from his heart" (that is, from the center of the affections) must become obedient to the standard of teaching to which the person is committed. I am pleased that Paul used the words "standard of teaching" here, for that connotes a wide range of action and ethical substance in relation to Christ as the goal of the "turned-around" person. And the term, "slave of righteousness" gives both the idea of work and the goal of work, namely, righteousness. Paul's concept of righteousness is similar in substance to Jesus' use of the term "kingdom of God."

Righteousness as the goal of a person's life is based on the theological affirmation that Christ is both the active agent and the example of what the Christian should be. In Paul's early life his parents, Judaism, and teachers such as Gamaliel formed the goal and content of his positive conscience; but after his inversion, Christ became the goal and content of his life. There are scores of direct citations in Paul's letters to illustrate this transformation. "Anyone who does not have the spirit of Christ does not belong to Him." (Romans 8:9); "Be imitators of me, as I am of Christ." (I Corinthians 11:1); "For we are the aroma of Christ to God among those who are being saved . . ." (II Corinthians 2:15); "If anyone is in Christ, he is a new creation; the old has passed away, behold the new has come." (II Corinthians 5:17); "I have been crucified with Christ; it is no longer I who live but Christ who lives in me; and the life I now live in the flesh I live by faith in the son of God, who loved me and gave himself for me." (Galatians 2:20)

The close link with shame as an emotional reaction if he did not live up to his vision of Christ is expressed by Paul in these words: "Yes, and I shall rejoice. For I know that through your prayers and the help of the Spirit of Jesus Christ this will turn out for my deliverances, as it is my eager expectation and hope that I shall not be at all ashamed, but that with full courage now as always Christ will be honored in my body, whether by life or by death. For to me to live is Christ, and to die is gain." (Philippians 1:19-21) Paul's letters are full of advice about the need for believers to live "in Christ"; and this meant making their decisions and even "marrying" in Christ.

Christ, to Paul, is far more than a divine personage who saves him from sin. Christ is the source and substance of his faith. With this theology, Christians are set on a course of righteousness. They are people with a program of things they want to do for God's glory. They are seekers after God's will for the world. Their only fear is of the shame that will come if they fail to live up to what they have voluntarily accepted as their goal, namely, the righteousness of God.

Lecture Four
Growth in Faith

Self-consciousness with its attending anxiety and hostility, we have said, leads to sinful acts that produce guilt. The self has a variety of strategies for handling guilt. Guilt functions through certain forms of religion. The completely developed conscience, however, also contains a positive element, and the Christian religion expects a personality "inversion" whereby Jesus Christ becomes the goal of faith. Now we must ask, "How does faith get started within a person and what should faith in Christ mean for a believer?"

THE EGO OF THE SELF

I have been using the word "self" as a general term for the whole inner reality of a person. Up to this point I have been discussing the formation and function of conscience. Now we must come to the conscious center of the self, the ego—that part of the self-system which observes, perceives,

79

thinks, wills, directs, schemes, plans, and is able to pass judgment.

The ego part of the self has been recognized since the days of the Greek philosophers as consisting of two parts: one part is the judge, the other part is judged; or, one part is a spectator and the other part is an actor in a drama. For our purposes, let us call the judge or spectator part of the ego the "I" and the judged or actor part of the ego the "Me."

One common way of thinking about the difference between the I and the Me is to say that the I is reason and the Me is emotion; or, the I is the mind at work in logical functions and the Me is the part that has been formed by interaction with other people. Looked at in this way, the I is nonhistorical and transcends the Me; the Me is connected to a particular society and rooted in specific actions which make up the person's history. Although this way of thinking about the dualism of the self is correct in that the ego is both the thing within that knows and the thing that is known, it is not satisfactory for our purposes. I have been assuming that the self as it unfolds and begins to function in its various parts does so in a cultural setting which the self in its totality absorbs. This means the I, as well as the Me, is culturally conditioned. A child growing up in an animist culture in Ethiopia will have an I that thinks animist thoughts, and these thoughts give a different understanding from that of a child growing up in a segment of a Western culture where physical causes are assumed for events that take place in nature. This being the case, we cannot say the I of the self is able to stand apart and judge impartially and non-historically any more than a Supreme Court judge can make judgments apart from the American culture and history of which he is a part.

H. Richard Niebuhr has summarized the matter in these words:

> The moral situation in which the self gives laws to itself, judges itself, approves or condemns itself is not one in which a higher self confronts a lower self but one in which a reasoning and feeling self takes toward itself the attitude of another which it represents to itself or which is presented to it![1]

In other words, we talk to ourselves. And what we talk about is how to be the kind of person we want to be in relation to the people and things about us. Psychologically speaking, supreme happiness is achieved when an individual's idea of himself or herself is matched by a social group's recognition of him or her as being that kind of person. Erikson uses these words:

> The sense of ego identity, then, is the accrued confidence that one's ability to maintain inner saneness and continuity (one's ego in the psychological sense) is matched by the saneness and continuity of one's meaning for

others. Thus, self-esteem, confirmed at the end of each major crisis, grows to be a conviction that one is learning effective steps toward a tangible future, that one is developing a defined personality within a social reality that one understands.[2]

The description of the process by which a person comes to a clear self-understanding and ego-certainty has no ethical connotation. The *process* is the same for making confirmed bank robbers as it is for producing Presbyterian ministers. Knowledge, discussed along these lines, is not abstract: on the contrary, it is personal. "Knowing" is an attempt to formulate theory or generalizations about the events of life that are satisfactory to the self and to the group or groups to which the self is related. The generalizations that are formed by the self, or the generalizations that are offered to the self which the self tests and finds to be true, then become "beliefs." As they are constantly tested by experience, beliefs are modified, redefined, or, in some cases, slowly discarded when they no longer function to relate the self to the world of experience. Moreover, this way of knowing is self-stimulating. The I has interests which it pursues, leaving other important things aside. The I has a system for deciding what is worth knowing, and it has an opinion about what it thinks it can know.

Conventional wisdom about human development assumed that the I of the self did not begin to function until children started to school or even later—during adolescence. Now we know through a wide range of research projects that the characteristics of the self which relate to I development are established early in a person's life. Benjamin S. Bloom has analyzed over a thousand different studies of the growth of small children, and his conclusions document this point. In brief, elements within the self such as trust, self-confidence, and initiative are fairly well established and functioning by age four, and these attitudes are the foundation of intellectual development.[3] Absorbed by the growing child from parents, these elements of personality are tools of the I as the child starts to control and shape his or her life. Thus, we see how the self is an inner reality but one that is deeply influenced by parents and other adults who nurture the growing child. Let us now examine the origin and development of faith as an attribute of the self.

There are two basic problems: first, the element of faith within the self, how it arises there; and second, the uniqueness—if any—of faith in God and how that is formed.

THE ELEMENT OF FAITH

Since our interest in developmental psychology is secondary to our concern for faith, we can suggest a solution to the first problem rather briefly. Erikson is the principal psychotherapist who has concerned himself with tracing the development of the ego through the whole life cycle, and he has said:

> For the first component of a healthy personality I nominate a sense of *basic trust*, which I think is an attitude toward oneself and the world, derived from the experiences of the first year of life. By "trust" I mean what is commonly implied in reasonable trustfulness as far as others are concerned and a simple sense of trustworthiness as far as oneself is concerned. When I say "basic," I mean that neither this component nor any of those that follow, are, either in childhood or adulthood, specially conscious. In fact, all of these criteria, when developed in childhood and when integrated in adulthood, blend into the total personality.[4]

Erikson continues by saying that by "sense of trust" he means the same thing we mean by "sense of health," and this "pervades surface and depth, consciousness and the unconscious." He traces the way the baby is nursed and handled to show how the baby in the first year learns to trust, to relate itself to the environment or else it learns some degree of mistrust. Furthermore, this knowing of trust or distrust will permeate the personality throughout life. In Erikson's thought the psychological term, "basic trust," is the same

thing as the religious term "faith." His language
is as follows:

> Whosoever says he has religion must derive a
> faith from it which is transmitted to infants
> in the form of basic trust; whosoever claims
> that he does not need religion must derive
> some basic faith from elsewhere.[5]

In Erikson's psychology, basic trust or faith is absolutely essential for human life, and its source is
the nurturing adults who handle the baby.

The second problem concerns the uniqueness—if any—of faith in God and how that is
formed. Erikson deliberately avoids the problem of
uniqueness, saying,

> It is not the psychologist's job to decide
> whether religion should or should not be con-
> fessed and practiced in particular words and
> rituals. Rather, the psychological observer
> must ask whether or not in any area under
> observation religion and tradition are living
> psychological forces creating the kind of faith
> and conviction which permeates a parent's
> personality and thus reinforces a child's basic
> trust in the world's trustworthiness.[6]

By keeping his eye on the human experience
of basic trust which develops a healthy personality, Erikson points out that millions of people

need the faith that religion can offer, that millions of people seem to get faith for this basic personality need without religion, and that millions who claim to have religion actually get mistrust from it. The important thing in this appraisal is the fact that faith and the sense of basic trust can be independent of religion.

Religion can foster faith and basic trust. This affirmation has been widely accepted in Protestant circles, and many leaders have been pleased to have such strong psychoanalytical support for religion as an ally of ego development. The opposite affirmation is also true: religion can create a climate of hate and fear so that parents communicate to their children a mistrust of themselves and their neighbors. There is, unfortunately, much evidence for this latter statement in the history of religious bigotry and wars. Moreover, we have all seen children who were dwarfed in their inner selves by the inflexible religious dogmas of their parents. We simply have to admit the truth of this observation and accept the judgment it implies. Indeed, some forms of religion crush the human spirit.

It is Erikson's other statement (that people can derive faith from experiences other than religion, such as "from friendship, productive work, social action, scientific pursuits, and artistic creation") which raises the theological issue more sharply. Is faith, then, simply a religious way to express what is first a good human characteristic—basic trust? If so, religion is just another category of human experience or another type of human association that may or may not be helpful in self-development. As a psychotherapist, this is as far as Erikson will go.

THE UNIQUENESS OF CHRISTIAN FAITH

We who hold to the Christian faith and use the Bible as our starting place for our thinking about religious matters must define for ourselves exactly what faith means.

Unique Object: God

The Christian's faith is in God. Although faith as a human characteristic may be analyzed psychologically, when God is affirmed to be the object of faith, then the nature of God is the decisive element. Broadly speaking, I believe God is spirit who created the world, sustains the people within it, and can give intelligible direction to human activity. This means that when individuals have faith in God, they will probably become maladjusted to some—if not major—portions of the present order of things. Even a casual reading of the Bible will indicate that people of faith set themselves against false religion as well as against religious institutions within Israel which had lost their sense of mission. Other people of faith reformed the meaning of religion when the accepted theology became inadequate. Prophets condemned the whole establishment of secular and religious leadership because they had a vision of what God wanted for Israel in a more equitable distribution of wealth. Sometimes the Biblical people of faith, such as John the Baptist, did not know what the future would be like. However, John knew that "even now the axe is laid to the root of the tree; every tree, therefore, that does not bear good fruit is cut down and thrown in the fire." (Matthew 3:10) If the God in whom we have faith is unique and not merely a prestigious and historically hollow term for all that is good in humankind then the meaning of faith is likewise unique.

Unique Goal: Communication with God

Psychologists have in mind some idea of what a normal person is like in order to treat and classify psychological disorders. The term itself implies that there is an order from which deviations can be identified. Generally speaking, psychologists have not been interested in trying to articulate their conception of health. Many were content to use Freud's broad characterization of a mentally healthy person as one who was able to love and to work.

Since World War II, psychologists and therapists have become more interested in the ego and in defining more precisely what a well integrated "whole" person is. Carl Rogers, for example, describes four such characteristics. (1) Openness to experience. A person is not defensive and has awareness of his or her own feelings and attitudes. Each new situation is taken as it is without the short-cut of categorizing. There is openness to new experience and therefore more realism in dealing with people. (2) Trust in one's organism. The person is able to trust the senses, instincts, memories; and all of these are available to help make practical decisions. There is more awareness of what causes mistakes and what can correct them. He or she has less fear and can handle more complex matters. (3) Internal locus of evaluation. More and more there is a realization that the locus of evaluation is within the self. The individual looks less and less to others and more to the creative ability he or she has. (4) Willingness to be a process. There is more willingness to be a process than a product. The immature person wants a fixed status with problems solved and anxieties allayed. The mature person can see the inner self in a single stream of "becoming." There is no need for mixed traits; one can be a continually changing constellation of potentialities.[7]

Abraham H. Maslow studied a group of people he thought showed mental health and formulated characteristics which describe what he called the "self-actualized" person. According to Maslow, these people had a more efficient perception of reality, an acceptance of their biological nature, a spontaneity of thought and action, an ability to focus on problems, an objectivity about themselves and their motives, an inner desire to grow without being too dependent on their environment, appreciation of normal human experiences—including the feeling that the world was a good place and that they could be useful in improving human life. Maslow continues his category of traits by saying the self-actualized person is capable of giving love, is friendly with all races, has a strong sense of ethical standards, an unhostile sense of humor, and creates in his or her own special way something from within the self.[8]

Maslow has more recently identified himself with a group of psychologists in what he labels "third force" psychology—to differentiate it from behaviorism on the one hand and from Freudianism on the other. "Third force" psychology claims to be going in a new direction because it has a new image of persons. This new image is that the human self has an *essence*, a character that is humanly *distinct* and that the goal of parents, teachers, and therapists should be to help a child become its true self. This statement seems so obvious to those of us who have an image of humanity as shaped by a religious tradition that we may fail to see how important this "third force" is. They are trying to see a person as being different from animals and as having power to develop a self that can rise above the forces which shaped the individual when it was a helpless baby. This approach requires an educational program which is highly individualized and which will incorporate momentous personal experiences of death, marriage and other "peak" experiences into one's selfhood.[9]

These major affirmations set "third-force" psychologists apart from other psychologists and give them a point of view very much like those of us who claim a religious orientation. Indeed, Maslow has used the resources of the Christian church to shape his psychology by citing St. Teresa and Meister Eckhardt as people who had had great mystical experiences and from these experiences had lifted the level of any individual's potential. It is important for our purpose to note that Maslow coined a phrase "peak experiences" to describe these great religious experiences in order to "secularize them and naturalize them."

The issue is clearly drawn. Maslow sees in religious experience human greatness, a power to break out of the cultural context which enslaves creativity and hampers human development. He describes the mystical experience as the finest possibility in life; then he separates it from the object of the experience—God—in order that it may be "naturalized." Then he is able to offer it as a model of what everyone should strive for. It is my contention that when the object of religious experience—God—is removed, the experience is not the same. Moses, Isaiah, and Paul did not have "peak experiences" to actualize their growing selfhood; rather, they had personal experiences with the living God. Their experiences did not lead them to self-development but to a sense of responsibility for God's people and of God's will for the world; and for this their lives were often in danger. Although we can describe the experience in humanistic terms, to leave the matter there is to omit the revelation of God—the one thing the Biblical prophets claim as the authority for their words and deeds.

Third-force psychologists have helped us, however, by their insistence that a person's self is the "locus of reality," that a person is capable of changing his or her life, and that decisions about events which form this life can be made in the light of the individual's experiences. Thus, the human mind is not forever chained to childhood experiences, nor is it conditioned by rewards and punishments as animals are so that it cannot strike out in new directions on its own.

Other psychologists who have studied the normal human life have not absolutized any form of normalcy. Rather, they have said that normalcy is something that has to be judged in the light of a person's whole history; and it certainly is not just a matter of the absence of mental disorders. Under this definition, conversion, mystical experiences, devotion, dedication to difficult causes which often threaten personal security can be appreciated for what they are rather than assuming that they are manifestations of some psychological pathology.

Having rejected the notion of psychological wholeness or the self-actualizing person as the *goal* of faith, what is the place of these concepts in the life of a person of faith?

My answer is that all parts of the self are affected by faith. The object of faith is God, and that experience modifies—to some extent—all the characteristics of the self. The degree of modification may not be great in some cases; in others it may be significant. For example, we may say the psychologically healthy person has compassion; but to whom is this compassion directed? Just to neighbors and friends? People of faith should begin to develop compassion for the poor and for others who have little social power or respectability and for people who cannot be expected to return the feeling of compassion. Faith in God sets up a tension within the self. The I of the self which judges and sets goals is informed by the image of Christ and puts pressure on the Me to change in the direction of the kind of activity Christ would sponsor. Thus, wholeness is a secondary consideration.

The primary consideration is communication with God, and this is done through worship and prayer. The theological background is explained by the writer of the book of Hebrews. The worship practices of Judaism required the priest to offer gifts and sacrifices of slain animals for the sins of the people. But these rituals of religion "cannot perfect the conscience of the worshippers" because they only take care of the guilt from the negative conscience (Hebrews 9:8-10). Calvin's

Commentary on this verse gets to the heart of the matter, for he says these rituals "did not reach the soul so as to confer true holiness." The writer to the Hebrews goes on to say that Christ has now become the high priest, "has entered once for all into the Holy Place, taking not the blood of goats and calves but his own blood, thus securing an eternal redemption." If the rituals of religion could save your conscience, how much more can Christ's sacrifice "purify your conscience from dead works to serve the living God"? (Hebrews 9:11-14) Faith in Christ opens up channels of communication with God who is concerned for the present and future.

Unique Program: Righteousness

Although many people will disagree with my concern to hold faith independent from—rather than dependent upon—psychological wholeness, more will be sympathetic to my contention that faith is somewhat independent of religion. I am using the word "religion" in this instance to mean the outward observable manifestations of a group who share common worship rites and have a common understanding of what their religion means. Faith experiences, of course, produce religion—just as the experiences of Moses and other leaders produced the major forms of worship and the central beliefs of the Hebrews. The experiences of Paul and the disciples produced the

Christian church and its beliefs. Contrariwise, religious groups produce persons of faith who alter the forms of religion. We shall discuss that process later. At this point I want to call attention to the problems of religion as a carrier of faith.

The record of religion as the generator and carrier of faith is not good. Viewed historically, organized institutional forms of religion seem to have tucked within themselves germs which in time spread a disease, lowering vitality and crippling their capacity to foster faith. Perhaps "germs" is not a good figure of speech, for germs come from outside the body; and it is my assumption that the disease which debilitates religion is caused by the way conscience is formed and is more like the loss of strength caused by aging. Because religion and conscience are both rooted in the experience of coming into self consciousness, religion tends to be a way to treat and handle the problems of the self. As indicated in Lecture III, there are many ways a person can manipulate the Christian belief system to solve the problems of conscience without opening the self to change or growth. Moreover, even in the Christian faith, no matter how fresh and clear God's revelation is to one person or to one generation, the theology of the revelation, when passed on to the children, becomes something they "ought" to believe rather than something they want to believe.

Thus, individuals tend to use religion to lessen the tension they feel within themselves rather than to open themselves to a relationship with God. Religion can supply satisfactory solutions to personal psychological problems, so there is little incentive to explore the Bible to find out exactly what faith in God means.

Institutions of religion are even more susceptible to this process of looking for satisfaction in things-as-they-are. Much of the Bible is an account of how God coached prophets and leaders to rekindle the fires of faith within the institutionalized forms of religion or to form new ones. Paul's letters to the churches he founded are full of admonitions about keeping the congregation instructed in the faith and resisting the corroding influences of the surrounding society (Romans 12:1; I Corinthians 1:17-31; Ephesians 4:17-25; I Thessalonians 4:1-13). As time went on, the problem became worse; this is illustrated in the way the officers in the congregation began to cater to the wealthy (James 2:1-5).

The reasons offered in the Bible for this condition are that people lost faith, turned from God, failed to repent or forgot their true heritage. We should not be surprised because institutions are established to perpetuate religion beyond the death of individuals and to inculcate religion in the young. The emphasis is on continuity, preservation, and adaptation to cultural and economic conditions. Leaders are selected who can keep order and enhance the power and prestige of their interpretation of past history. This type of leader proves himself or herself by making an accommodation to economic, political, and even military power. Almost by definition, religious institutions are allergic to anything which changes or challenges the status quo.

One of the reasons we do not see these liabilities in religion is that we in America are still enthralled with pietism and an extreme form of individualism. We tend to believe that if individual Christians would just read and absorb the First and Twenty-third Psalms, the 13th Chapter of I Corinthians and a few other classical devotional passages, they would be able to make radical changes in themselves and in society. Why is it that we seldom urge people to read and ponder Matthew, Chapter 23? Matthew's report of Jesus' speaking to his disciples and to the crowds is a mirror held up to the religious situation of all ages.

Jesus lashed out at the established leaders of Judaism. Why? Not because they had committed any of the usual sins—such as stealing, lying, or immoral sexual activity—but because of their sins of attitude. Jesus berated them for the way they let Judaism drift. The religious leaders preached but did not practice. They assigned responsibility to others but did nothing themselves. They reveled in their costumes and the deference paid them. They were meticulous about tithes but paid no attention to justice and mercy. Jesus concluded his attack and made his most stinging denunciation when he said the leaders would "build the tombs of the prophets and adorn the monuments of the righteous, saying, 'If we had lived in the days of our fathers, we would not have taken part with them in shedding the blood of the prophets.' " Jesus exposed that pious nonsense by saying that he would send prophets and wise men and that these religious leaders would beat and persecute some of them, killing others. Then his lamentation, "Oh, Jerusalem, Jerusalem, killing the prophets and stoning those who were sent to you! How often would I have gathered your children together as a hen gathers her brood under her wings, and you would not! Behold, your house is forsaken and desolate." (Matthew 23:27)

I accept Matthew 23 as a highly condensed version of what happens to religion as it drifts from one generation to another. It tends to lose contact with God while finding connections and alliances with the power structures of society. Someone put it this way: religion seldom improves with age!

One could take Matthew 23 and turn it around, so to speak, and have a remarkable identification of what Jesus thought religious faith could be and what religious leaders should be like. They should have a life that is in harmony with their preaching and teaching; they should be servants to the needs of humanity and move about without ostentation; they should be responsible for each other and all under God, the teacher. I need not translate all of Jesus' criticisms into their positive expectation in order to make the point that religion in its vital form is concerned with a program of activities as well as the equilibrium of the self. Jesus pointed this out in a forceful way in his first sermon in his home synagogue. He said he was going to fulfill the Messianic program which had been outlined in Isaiah 61:1-2; and this so enraged the religious people that they attempted to throw him out of the city (Luke 4:16-19; 28-30).

Almost everywhere in the Bible where we have a claim of God's revelation, we have God's program for the chosen people. In the earliest stories it was God's desire that people live in harmony, but they would not; and Noah was selected to save the human race from the flood because he was "righteous" (Genesis 6:7-9). Moses' program was to lead the people out of Egypt, but he was by no means anxious to undertake this venture (Exodus 3:13—4:31). The stories of the kings of Israel, especially David and Solomon, are told against the background of what God wanted them to do and their efforts either to compromise God's desire or their outright disobedience. The latter part of the book of Isaiah is full of the sins of Israel and the resulting doom that is to come. The Old Testament prophets give us a picture of both the weaknesses of formal religion on the one hand and the program of God for his people on the other. We can read these passages and see the differences between religion and faith. For example, God, according to Micah, would not be pleased with the regular approaches of bowing-down, burnt offerings, even rivers of oil as offerings. According to Micah, one could not even gain favor with God by sacrificing his first-born child. Micah put the program in these words: "He has showed you, Oh man, what is good; and what does the Lord require of you but to do justice, and to love kindness, and to walk humbly with your God?" (Micah 6:8).

GROWTH IN FAITH

My purpose in this essay is to show that conscience—as it develops in an individual—is most often allied with religion because both are formed in the process of becoming self-conscious. Moreover, the family into which each individual is born already has a religion and a moral code. Through natural processes already discussed, the child incorporates the particular form of religion and morals which is "ready-at-hand." Most people live out their whole lives with only slight modifications of what they accepted as a child.

My thesis is that the accepted form of religion and morals must be inverted through an experience with Christ. Normally, this will not occur until adolescence or later because it requires mature judgment and entails taking responsibility for growing in faith. Most of this lecture has been a discussion of what faith means in contrast to religion. Now let us identify what is involved when an individual grows in faith.

Testing Established Beliefs

In order to grow in faith, one must test established beliefs. Such testing does not mean abandoning a belief but finding its truth for one's self. The tension that exists between faith and formal beliefs and ecclesiastical organizations developed by previous generations is a mark of spiritual health.

Faith works in and through and sometimes against religion in order to create or restore contact with God. So, reformation of religion should be the normal expectation of Christians, especially Protestants who were in a state of revolt in various parts of the world for several hundred years after Luther's lifetime. But the drift away from God is no respecter of the claims of any religion. Protestantism, although it had its birth in revolt, soon drifted to hard dogmas in some countries—especially in Holland and New England—and today finds itself not so much encrusted with dogma as allied in subtle ways with the powerful and the privileged in our society.

Harnack's thesis—that Christianity is, in its center, an "energy" which became encrusted in time with dogma that choked out the dynamism of God's spirit—may be overdone. But the evidence is on Harnack's side that, at the Reformation, the Christian church had become something vastly different from the church described in the

New Testament literature. But whether against encrusted dogma, privileged position in society, or ecclesiastical authority, faith is the dynamic element which seeks to enliven and refresh the believer.

Living on the Basis of Beliefs

Faith is often thought to be a vague, indefinite impulse that activates saints and martyrs but is seldom seen in ordinary people. This is probably because the Bible and church historians have attributed to the great leaders of the Judeo-Christian tradition a special amount of faith. But this impression is false. Faith is not vague, nor is it limited to famous leaders. On the contrary, faith is precise. People of faith, according to Biblical accounts, were expected to do exact and practical things. The model for the church is the Gospel account of Jesus and his disciples. For example, Jesus saw Peter and Andrew fishing and he said, "Follow me and I will make you fishers of men" (Matthew 4:19). It is this precise nature of faith which makes it startling. We know that throughout the Bible the testimony is the same: when a person comes to know God, his or her life is changed in a specific and practical way. So, I would contend that it is the precision of faith that really worries us.

This practicality is not only a matter of changing our lifestyle; it is also related to the program that faith entails. This program is shown by Biblical accounts as being so specific that auditors hearing the program, even though they might be religious, usually rejected it. But the point is not the rejection or rage of "status quo" people. The point for our purpose is that faith is fused to action and can be seen and evaluated. Faith in that sense is objective. Because this program is about matters which affect the daily lives of people, it is political in the sense that it is an honest attempt to change the existing order in spite of opposition. It is impossible to think of faith in Biblical terms without thinking about conflicts with personal desires, social practices, ecclesiastical authority, or political order. Faith by definition is a conviction that life should be changed because the believer has seen what God wants for a specific time and place.

Training the I To Domesticate the Me

These observations then lead us back to the question of the self. If faith is unique in goal and program, then it must be related to the I of the self—the I of the conscious, rational, purposeful, willing part of the self-system. For this reason it is also the part of the self that is open to communication from the outside, to correction and to guidance. On the surface this affirmation seems so conventional that perhaps I should indicate more precisely what it means.

Many psychologists and theologians hold the position that God is present in a person in some latent way deep within the personality. Aided by the Jungian analysis that there is a racial unconscious which transcends culture and the notion of the archetype images which are implanted deep within the unconscious mind, it is affirmed that the conscious appropriation of God is the natural outworking of the God archetype. Jung as a psychologist refused to make this connection, but others have done so.

The trouble with this position is that it means so little. The meaning of *God* can be understood only in human behavior. There are so many God-concepts in the world with such diverse meaning that I see no reason to search for a God-archetype, since the archetype gives no common form to religion. The notion of self-consciousness as the rootage for religion is just as satisfactory as a general locale for religion, and it makes possible a more specific analysis as I have attempted to show in these lectures. Also, Jungian psychology is intent on establishing wholeness as a personal goal and thus intensifying the search within the self to such an extent that one writer can say, "Holiness is wholeness."[10] Rather, holiness is obedience. Wholeness is subordinate to the goal of faith, which is God, and to the program of faith, which is God's will for humanity.

On the other hand, this notion that faith is connected with the I of the self does not mean a rationalistic faith. Rational categories do not

dominate faith, and faith is not limited to the I of
the self. It does not mean that faith is logical or
that faith comes from the mind. The person of
faith knows what is believed and what the goal is.
The person's mind functions toward the object of
faith—God. The I is constantly surveying, coach-
ing, condemning and encouraging the Me of the
self, which in turn is connected to the unconscious
parts of the mind and to the instincts. What is
being said is that the I is in a struggle to dominate, to domesticate, and to direct the Me. In that
sense, the I is dealing with the whole nonrational
apparatus of the self, but it is trying to do it in a
reasonable way.

We must grant that the I is not very strong;
but it is persistent and it can obtain allies in its
struggle. The principal ally is a group of friends
who share similar notions of what the I should be.
Such a group provides endorsement and rein-
forcement of an I which is objective, that is, which
can be discussed and formulated in mental images, in actions that are approved for recurring
human situations or for actions that are projected
in hypothetical situations as authentic ways for
the commonly held I to function.

Rather than making faith rationalistic, this
is a way of being rational about faith. It no more
ignores the nonrational or the unconscious part of
the mind than does psychiatry. Although there
are many different therapies used in psychiatry, a
basic one is conversation in which the therapist,
through the I of the self, helps the troubled self

become more aware of the reasons for its difficulty and provides a relationship on which the I can rely while the whole self is being treated. Psychotherapy, which deals with the self and the nonrational parts of the self, is one of the most rational of sciences. Faith, likewise, deals with the whole self; but it is connected to the self through the I, and its activity can be evaluated as well as any human activity can be analyzed.

A GIFT FROM GOD

Faith, then, is subjective—an inward, introspective finding of oneself; but the truth about ourselves is objective in the sense that it lies beyond us and is not subject to our control. "You have not chosen me but I have chosen you" is the order of one's experience, according to John (John 15:16). The truth that seeks us comes through a person, Jesus Christ.

The objectivity of God's communication to persons is universally observed in Biblical people. The voice is not from the community. It is not a person's conscience or his idealized concept of what ought to be. It is a voice from beyond time which makes personal time meaningful and precious. When known as the object of faith, God is not known first as having a concern for persons in general but as having concern for me in my time and in my condition. This radical affirmation of God defies logical reason. The receiver of faith from God never knows the reason for being visited, is never able to justify God's gift of grace. The experience is so shattering of complacency that one's previously held self-image is destroyed. The receiver either suddenly or slowly begins to understand the self in a new light; the former life with its fears and frustrations is dissolved, and a new being begins to grow toward the object of faith, God. It is the same world to be sure, and the person is still held in the same body with its appetites and glandular needs; but the outlook is different. The individual becomes reoriented—the center of life is Christ, and all that radiates from that center is reorganized and charged with fresh significance. Paul expresses the experience with these words, ". . . if any one is in Christ he is a new creation; the old has passed away, behold the new has come" (II Corinthians 5:17).

The writer of the letter to the Ephesians said in two verses most of what I have been saying in these lectures.

For by grace you have been saved through faith; and this is not your own doing; it is a gift of God—not because of works, lest any man should boast. For we are his workmanship, created in Christ Jesus for good works, which God prepared beforehand, that we should walk in them. (Ephesians 2:8-10)

Notes

1. Reinhold Niebuhr, *The Nature and Destiny of Man* (New York: Charles Scribner's Sons, 1947), Vol. I, p. 182.
2. Alfred M. Rehwinkel, *The Voice of Conscience* (St. Louis: Concordia Publishing House, 1956), pp. 22-23. See also Carl F. H. Henry, *Christian Personal Ethics* (Grand Rapids: Wm. B. Eerdmans Publishing Co., 1957), p. 519.
3. O. Hallesby, *Conscience* (Minneapolis: Augsburg Publishing House, 1933), pp. 12-13.
4. Frederick Denison Maurice, *The Conscience* (London: Macmillan and Co., 1883), p. 27.

Lecture Two

1. Sigmund Freud, *On Narcissism: An Introduction* (London: Hogarth Press, 1957), pp. 30-59.
2. Robert R. Sears, Lucy Ran, and Richard Alpert, *Identification and Child Rearing* (Palo Alto, California: Stanford University Press, 1965), p. 260.
3. *Ibid.*, p. 3.

Lecture Three

1. Robert K. Merton, *Social Theory and Social Structure* (New York: The Free Press, Revised and

Enlarged Edition, 1957), pp. 19-84. See especially pp. 60-72.

2. C. A. Pierce, *Conscience in the New Testament* (Chicago: Alec R. Allenson, Inc., 1955).

Lecture Four

1. H. Richard Niebuhr, "The Ego-Alter Dialectic and the Conscience," Journal I of Philosophy, XLII (June 21, 1945), p. 355.

2. Erik H. Erikson, "Identity and the Life Cycle," *Psychological Issues*, Vol. I, No. I, 1959, p. 89.

3. Benjamin S. Bloom, *Stability and Change in Human Characteristics* (New York: John Wiley, 1965).

4. Erikson, *op. cit.*, pp. 55-56.

5. *Ibid.*, p. 65.

6. *Ibid.*, p. 64.

7. C. E. Moustakas, *The Self, Explorations in Personal Growth* (New York: Harper and Brothers, 1956), p. 125.

8. *Ibid.*, p. 160.

9. Abraham H. Maslow, "Some Educational Implications of the Humanistic Psychologies," *Harvard Educational Review*, Vol. 38, No. 4, Fall, 1968, p. 685. See also *Toward a Psychology of Being* (Princeton: D. Van Nostrand Co., 1962).

10. Josef Goldbrunner, *Holiness Is Wholeness* (New York: Pantheon, 1955).